# THE LIGHT OF CLARIFICATION AND SALVATION OF THE SOULS

# نور الإيضاح ونجاة الأرواح

Marifah Press,
IG: marifahpress
info@marifahinstitute.com



ISBN 9781915025791

Translation: Bilal Brown
Cover design & typesetting: Imran Rahim • enquiries@ethereadesign.com

# Contents

TRANSLITERATION KEY

| | | | |
|---|---|---|---|
| ḍ | ض | ‘ | ء(أإ) |
| ṭ | ط | a, ā | ا |
| ẓ | ظ | b | ب |
| a, ‘i, ‘u’ ,’ | ع | t | ت |
| gh | غ | th | ث |
| f | ف | j | ج |
| q | ق | ḥ | ح |
| k | ك | kh | خ |
| l | ل | d | د |
| m | م | dh | ذ |
| n | ن | r | ر |
| h | ه | z | ز |
| w, u, ū | و | s | س |
| y, i, ī | ي | sh | ش |
| | | ṣ | ص |

# Preface

All praise belongs to Allah the one who gives knowledge and understanding to whoever He wills and peace and blessings of Allah be upon the most honourable of His creation, the master of mankind, Muhammad bin Abdullah and upon his family, companions, and all those you follow him in a good manner.

I undertook the task of translating this primer in jurisprudence of the Hanafi school of law, having studied it three times with different teachers and taught it multiple times thereafter. The text is widely accepted and taught in the Hanafi Muslim world and is usually a starting point for the student of sacred knowledge. The two previous translations that I came across were beneficial, but amalgamated with additional commentary from the translators and strayed from the original wording at times, making it difficult to focus solely on the primary text. I hope that this translation will be of benefit to the student of knowledge and I have added space at the bottom of each page for recording notes when studying with a teacher.

I have attempted to remain as loyal as possible to the original text, which may cause some difficulty in understanding due to the brevity of the text (this is also experienced with the original Arabic text). In order to aid comprehension, I have added footnotes which are mainly from the author's own commentary *Maraqi al-Falah*, from *Radd al-Muhtar*, *Hashiyah al-Tahtawi*, and *Al-Muhit al-Burhani*.

I also used the male pronoun instead of a gender-neutral one to remain loyal to the text, even though the rulings apply to male and female alike unless stated otherwise.

I ask Allah سبحانه وتعالى to allow everyone who reads it to understand and benefit from it and that he places it as a barrier between me and the Hellfire in the Hereafter.

## Biography of Imam al-Shurunbulali

His name is Hasan bin Ammar bin Ali al-Shurunbulali, in relation to Shubra Bilulah in the Menofia Governorate in Egypt. He was born in 994 AH (1586 CE). His father took him to Cairo at the age of six and he busied himself with studying the sacred sciences and memorisation of the Quran. He went to Al-Azhar University and studied until he become one the prominent jurists of his time and the one relied upon for issuing fatwas. He busied himself teaching and authoring books until his dying day. He authored Nur al-Idah in the year 1032 AH and then wrote a commentary on it named Imdad al-Fattah that he completed in the year 1046 AH. He then summarised Imdad al-Fattah in the book named Maraqi al-Falah in the year 1054 AH. He passed away on Friday after the afternoon prayer on 21st Ramadan in the year 1069 AH (1659 CE). May Allah have mercy on his soul.

## Glossary of Terms

### TYPES OF LEGAL RULINGS

#### *Farḍ* (Obligatory)

This action has been established by unquestionable evidence. Examples include the five obligatory prayers and fasting in Ramadan. Rejection of this is unbelief, but leaving it without a valid excuse is sinful and deserving of punishment in the Hereafter. Integrals of an action are from this category and will render the action null and void if missed.

#### *Wājib* (Necessary)

This action has been established by probabilistic evidence. Examples include the Witr prayer and the two Eid prayers. Rejection of this is not unbelief, but leaving it without a valid excuse is also sinful and deserving of punishment. Non-integral obligations of an action are from this category that do not render the action completely null and void.

#### *Sunnah* [*Mu'akkadah*] (Emphasised Practice)

This is an action regularly practiced by the Prophet ﷺ or the rightly guided caliphs (Allah be pleased with them) after him. It is not necessary, but could be close in rank to necessary if it is from the symbols of the religion. Leaving it continuously or entirely without an excuse could be deemed as being serious and worthy of chastisement. Examples include the adhan and saying at least three glorifications in each prostration of the prayer.

*Mustaḥabb, Mandūb, Adab, Faḍīlah, Sunnah Ghayru Mu'akkadah* **(Recommended)**

This is an action liked and preferred by the Sacred Law, but it is not necessary. Examples include the forenoon prayer and fasting the 10th of Muharram. There is reward entailed in performing it but no sin or blame in leaving it.

Obligatory, necessary and sunnah actions can each be categorised into *personal* and *communal.*

Personal is an action sought from every legally responsible person. Examples of each type include performing the five obligatory daily prayers, Witr prayer, and the prayer in congregation.

Communal is an action sought from a group of legally responsible people. The duty is removed from the group if some of them, even one, perform the action. However, the reward for performing the action is only for those individuals who performed it. Any sin or blame, though, for leaving it is on the group collectively. Examples of each type include the funeral prayer, responding to a greeting and spiritual retreat in the last ten days of Ramadan.

*Ḥarām* **(Prohibited)**

This is an action that has been made prohibited by unquestionable evidence. Anyone who deems it lawful is an unbeliever, but performing the action is sinful and deserving of punishment. Examples include adultery and drinking wine.

*Makrūh Taḥrīmī* **(Prohibitively Disliked)**

This is an action that has been made prohibited based on probabilistic evidence and is closer to the haram. Whoever deems it permissible is *not* an unbeliever, but performing the action is also sinful and deserving of punishment. Examples include women praying alone in a group together and fasting on Eid.

*Makrūh Tanzīhī* **(Mildly Disliked)**

This is closer to permissibility. Leaving the action is best and rewardable and performing the action is disliked by the Sacred Law but with no sin or punishment. Examples include repeating the same chapter in both units of the obligatory prayer and wasting water in wudu.

*Mubāh, Jā'iz, Lā Ba's, Halal* **(Permitted)**

This is an action that there is no command to perform nor prohibition by the Sacred Law. There is no reward in performing the action and equally there is no sin in leaving it. Examples include wiping over leather socks or using a dry toothbrush whilst fasting.

## QIYĀS VS ISTIḤSĀN

### *Qiyās* (Analogy)

Qiyās is to attach the legal ruling of a matter that has not been mentioned scripturally to the ruling of a matter that has been mentioned scripturally because of them sharing the legal cause of the ruling. For example, the Quran has prohibited buying and selling after the call to prayer on Fridays[1], this can be extended to rental contracts, loans, and all other contracts due to the joint legal cause which is "being busied and distracted from the Friday sermon and prayer." There are several conditions for applying qiyās and it must undergo rigorous testing and scrutiny before being applied.

### *Istiḥsān* (Legal Discretion)

Istiḥsān is an overriding of analogy due to the presence of a stronger proof, or it is diverting from giving the ruling in a particular scenario with the same ruling that was given to its equivalents, to giving a ruling that is opposed to it because of a stronger aspect that necessitates diverting from the first one. Only four types are mentioned in Hanafi texts[2]:

#### 1. Istiḥsān due to scriptural evidence (*naṣṣ/athar*)

For example, the general rule that the Sacred Law has set is that it is prohibited to sell something that you don't have in your possession. However, the Messenger of Allah ﷺ allowed an advanced payment contract and said: "*Whoever carries out an advanced payment purchase for dates, then let him do it with a known volume and a known weight.*"[3]

Due to the presence of scripture, analogy is overridden (due to it having a greater possibility of error) and the scripture is implemented.

#### 2. Istiḥsān due to mutual agreement (*ijmāʿ*)

This means that the widespread agreed upon practice of the Muslims from the time of the Prophet ﷺ until the present contradicts the general rule based on analogy. An example of the rental of a public bath (hammam), the general rule that the Sacred Law has set is that it is prohibited to lease something

1 Quran: 62:9.

2 Some contemporary scholars have erroneously added other types.

3 Al-Bukhari (2239).

that the amount and time of it is unknown. However, due to the widespread practice of paying to use public baths, the analogy is overridden due to the high possibility of it being erroneous and a weaker proof.

### 3. Istiḥsān due to necessity (*ḍarūrah*)

This is when the analogy places people in hardship. For example, the remnant water of a predatory bird is impure by analogy. However, due to them swooping down from above and it being unavoidable, the analogy is overridden and the water is deemed to be pure but disliked. Another example is the permissibility of rental contracts due to the need of people to conduct them even though the exact usufruct does not exist at the time of the contract.

### 4. Istiḥsān due to subtle analogy (*qiyās khafiy*)

This is when two analogies clashed, one of them is apparent and the other is subtle but is a stronger proof in the view of that particular scholar. The majority of istiḥsān is of this type. An example of this is if a buyer and a seller have a dispute regarding the amount of payment that was taken, analogy dictates that the buyer should win the case (by swearing an oath) because the seller is making a claim of extra (the payment) and the buyer is negating it. However, istiḥsān dictates that they both swear an oath because the buyer is making the claim against the seller the obligation of handing the item over to him and taking the lesser payment. It is called a subtle analogy because its ruling can be applied to other cases such as leasing and marriage. Another example is someone who is unconscious for five prayers or less, he must make them up. Qiyās dictates that he should not make any prayers up if his unconsciousness lasts an entire prayer time due to his inability to pray, so it resembles insanity from this aspect. However, istiḥsān dictates that because the missed prayers are few, there is no hardship in making them up,[4] so it resembles the one who has been asleep from this aspect.

Istiḥsān is mostly applied over qiyās in the Hanafi School, but on rare occasions, qiyās is given preference.

---

4 Al-Hidayah, Chapter of the Prayer of the Sick Person.

# The Light of Clarification
## AND SALVATION OF THE SOULS

# The Book of Purification

The types of water that are permissible[1] for purification are seven types:

1. Rainwater.
2. Seawater.
3. Water from a river[2].
4. Water from a well.
5. Water from melted snow and
6. Hail.
7. Springwater.[3]

Thereafter, water is divided into five categories[4]:

1. Pure, purifying, and *not* disliked i.e. "unrestricted" water.
2. Pure, purifying, and disliked i.e. that from which a cat[5] drank and what is analogous to it[6] providing it is a small amount[7].
3. Pure and not purifying i.e. that which has been used to remove legal impurity (*al-Ḥadath*)[8] or for an act of worship like wudu

1 i.e. valid to use.

2 This includes streams and canals.

3 This method of categorisation is not the norm in the Hanafi texts (which always start with the obligatory aspects of wudu) and it seems that Al-Shurunbulali has borrowed it from the Shafi'i texts namely, "Al-Ghayah wa al-Taqrib".

4 Again, this logical categorisation is something borrowed from the Shafi'i texts.

5 A domestic cat [Maraqi al-Falah, page 13].

6 The cat.

7 Meaning the body of water is small not the amount drank, this will be discussed later on, but should have been mentioned first.

8 Even without intention.

on top of wudu with intention. Water becomes "used" with mere separation from the body. It is not permitted[9] to make wudu with sap or fruit juice even if the sap/juice exits by itself without being squeezed according to the stronger view[10] nor with water that its nature has been removed by cooking or the overpowering of something else over it.

Overpowering with the mixing of solids is with the removal of the water from its thinness and viscosity. The changing of all of its properties[11] with a solid[12] such as saffron, fruit, or tree leaves causes no harm.

Overpowering with liquids is with the appearance of one property from a liquid that only has two properties, such as milk, which has colour and taste and has no smell,[13] and with the appearance of two properties from a liquid that has three properties such as vinegar[14]. Overpowering with a liquid that has no property, such as "used" water and rosewater whose smell has dissipated, is by weight. So, if two *riṭl* of "used" water are mixed with one *riṭl*[15] of "unrestricted" water then wudu is not permitted with it, but the opposite is permitted.

4. The fourth is impure water i.e. that which an impurity has landed in and is still and small. Small is what is less than ten by ten[16], so it

---

9 i.e. not valid.

10 As opposed to what is mentioned in Al-Hidayah in the Chapter of Purification and Tabyin al-Haqa'iq in the Chapter of Purification.

11 The smell, taste, and colour.

12 That becomes mixed without cooking [Maraqi al-Falah, page 15].

13 Generally, it has no strong smell unless it is going bad.

14 Smell, colour, and taste

15 An archaic measurement roughly 380g/380ml of water.

16 Ten arms lengths. This is measured from the tip of the finger to the elbow which

........................................................................................................................

........................................................................................................................

........................................................................................................................

........................................................................................................................

........................................................................................................................

........................................................................................................................

........................................................................................................................

........................................................................................................................

will become impure even if the trace doesn't appear in it, or flowing but the trace of it[17] appears in it. Trace is *taste, colour*, or *smell*.

5. The fifth is doubtful water in relation to its purifying[18] i.e. that from which a donkey or hinny[19] drank.

---

is roughly 46cm. What is mentioned here is not the position of Abu Hanifah or Abu Yusuf, it has been narrated from Imam Muhammad (and other things have been narrated from him). Whereas Abu Hanifah does not make any estimation and said that small and large depends on what the person looking at the water believes to be small or large. See: [Al-Muhit al-Burhani, Chapter of Purification, Section Four concerning waters that wudu is permitted with].

17 The impurity.

18 Not its purity.

19 The mother of a hinny is a donkey and the father is a horse [Maraqi al-Falah, page 17].

........................................................................................................

........................................................................................................

........................................................................................................

........................................................................................................

........................................................................................................

........................................................................................................

........................................................................................................

........................................................................................................

## Section of Clarifying the Rules of Remnant Water

If an animal drinks from a small amount of water then it is divided into four categories and called "remnant":

1. The first is pure and purifying i.e. that from which a human being, horse[20], or that whose meat is consumed[21] drank.
2. The second is impure, not permitted to use i.e. that from which a dog, pig, or a thing[22] from the beasts of prey like a leopard and a wolf drank.
3. The third is that which usage of it is disliked[23] when other water is available i.e. the remnant water of a cat[24], free-range chicken[25], birds of prey such as a hawk, falcon, and a kite, "inhabitants of houses" such as a mouse not a scorpion.

---

20 Horse is mentioned specifically here due to a difference of opinion as regards to the permissibility of eating its meat, it has been said that its remnant water is doubtful, impure, and disliked respectively.

21 Lawful animals, like cows, goats, sheep, and camels etc.

22 Meaning "an animal" [Maraqi al-Falah, page 19].

23 Mildly disliked [ibid.].

24 A domestic cat, not a wild one [ibid.].

25 The dislike is due to the chicken pecking around in the filth and uncertainty of the cleanliness of its beak thereafter, this can occur with barn chickens too. See: [ibid.].

........................................................................................................

........................................................................................................

........................................................................................................

........................................................................................................

........................................................................................................

........................................................................................................

........................................................................................................

........................................................................................................

4. The fourth is doubtful in relation to its purifying i.e. the remnant water of a hinny and a donkey, so if one does not find anything else then they make wudu with it and *tayammum*[26] then pray.

26 See Section of Tayammum.

## Section of Investigation[27]

If containers become mixed up[28] when the majority of them are pure, one investigates for wudu and drinking. However, if the majority are impure then one does not investigate except for drinking. With garments that are mixed up, one investigates whether the majority are pure or impure.

---

27 Meaning to exercise one's judgement, which is *the expenditure of effort to attain the objective* [Maraqi al-Falah, page 138].

28 Side by side, not the water [Maraqi al-Falah, page 21].

## Section of Matters Pertaining to Wells

A small[29] well is drained with

1. the falling of an impurity even if it is small (not from dung) like a drop of blood or wine,
2. the falling of a pig, even if it comes out alive and its snout did not touch the water,
3. the dying of a dog[30], sheep, or human being in it, and with
4. the inflating of an animal even if it is small.

Two-hundred buckets are drained if it cannot be drained[31]. If a chicken or a cat or something similar[32] to them dies in it, then forty buckets must be removed. If a mouse or what is analogous[33] to it dies in it, then twenty buckets must be removed. It will be a purification for the well, the bucket, the rope, and the hand of the person who draws the water.

---

29 The amount of small has already been defined, see Section of Clarifying the Rules of Remnant Water

30 The reason a dog is mentioned is that it is not intrinsically impure like a pig. A note should be made here that a dog does not sweat via its main body, rather, panting is the most efficient way dogs have to cool themselves, so as long as the nose or tongue has not been in contact with the water it will be considered as pure water unless known otherwise. See: [Maraqi al-Falah, page 23].

31 Completely.

32 In size.

33 In size.

........................................................................................................

........................................................................................................

........................................................................................................

........................................................................................................

........................................................................................................

........................................................................................................

........................................................................................................

........................................................................................................

A well does not become impure with droppings[34], manure[35], or dung[36] unless the onlooker deems it a lot or that a bucket is not free of a dropping. Water is not ruined with pigeon or sparrow droppings, nor with the death of that which has no blood[37] in it[38] such as a fish, frog, aquatic animal, bedbug[39], fly, wasp, and scorpion, nor with the falling of a human or animal whose meat is edible[40] if it comes out alive and there is no impurity its body, nor with the falling of a mule, donkey, birds of prey, or wild animal[41] according to the correct stance[42]. If the saliva of the fallen thing comes into contact with the water, then it[43] takes its[44] ruling[45]. The presence of a dead animal in it[46] will make it impure from a day and night, and an inflated animal from three days and three nights[47] if the time of its falling is not known.

---

34 From camels, goats, and sheep [Maraqi al-Falah, page 24].
35 From horses, donkeys, and mules [ibid.].
36 From cows and buffaloes [ibid.].
37 Flowing blood [Maraqi al-Falah, page 25].
38 In the water or liquid.
39 *Cimex lectularius.*
40 Such as camels, sheep etc.
41 Like a lion or a monkey etc.
42 It was said that the water needs to be removed, but this is a weaker opinion.
43 The water.
44 The saliva.
45 See Section of Tayammum.
46 The well.
47 72 hours.

## Section of *al-Istinjā'*

*Al-istibrā'*[48] is binding for a man,[49] until the trace of urine disappears and his heart is content, according to his habit, by either walking, coughing, lying down, or another method. Initiation of wudu is not permitted[50] for him to until he is content with the disappearance of the wetness of the urine. *Al-istinjā'* from an impurity that exits the front or rear passage is sunnah[51] as long as it does not go past the orifice. If it does go past and it is[52] the amount of the *dirham*[53] then it is *wājib*[54] to remove it with water. If it is more than the *dirham* then it is *farḍ* to wash it. It is *farḍ* to wash that which is in the orifice at the time of washing from major legal impurity (*al-janābah* [55]), menstruation, and postpartum bleeding even if what is on the orifice is a small amount. In addition, he performs[56] *al-istinjā'* with a purifying stone[57]and what is simi-

48 *Al-istibrā'* is to make sure that the front orifice is free of wetness from urine [Maraqi al-Falah, page 27].

49 The opposite understanding is that it is not binding for a woman [ibid.].

50 i.e. Not valid [ibid.]

51 A confirmed sunnah for men and women [ibid.].

52 Exactly.

53 The *dirham* discussed here is not the same as the one used for zakah rather it is what is called *al-dirham al-mithqāli* which is the equivalent of a *mithqāl* (4.25g) [Maraqi al-Falah, page 28].

54 Not *farḍ* and it can no longer be called *al-istinjā'* [Maraqi al-Falah, page 28].

55 This could be due to a nocturnal emission (a wet dream), masturbation with ejaculation or vaginal/anal penetration without ejaculation.

56 It is sunnah to do so [Maraqi al-Falah, page 28].

57 Not a coarse stone like a brick nor smooth and bare like a gemstone, the point

lar to it[58] but washing with water is liked more and the best thing is joining between water and stones, so he will wipe then wash. It is permitted for him to restrict himself to water or stones. The sunnah is cleaning of the area and the number of stones is recommended and not a confirmed (*mu'akkadah*) sunnah, so he performs *al-istinjā'* with three stones as a recommendation if cleaning is attained with less than them.

The method[59] of *al-istinjā'* is to wipe from the direction of the front to the back with the first stone, from the back to the front with the second, and from the front to the back with the third if the testicles are low-hanging. If they are not low-hanging, then he starts from the back to the front. A woman starts from the front to the back out of fear of staining her vagina. He then washes his hand initially with water then rubs the area with water using the inside of a finger or two or three if he needs to. A man raises[60] his middle finger above the others at the beginning of *al-istinjā'* then he raises his ring finger[61] and he doesn't restrict himself to one finger. A woman raises her ring finger and middle finger together initially out of fear of attaining excitement[62]. He exaggerates in cleaning until the foul smell ends and in relaxing his bottom

---

is purification [Maraqi al-Falah, page 28].

58 Toilet paper is sufficient in our day and age.

59 The goal is cleaning and purification and no specific detailed method has been recorded in the Shariah therefore whichever method is closer to purity is recommended, thus the embarrassing detail can be spared. Imam al-Haskafi says in al-Durr al-Mukhtar, "It is not restricted to wiping forward in the winter and backward in the summer." See: [Radd al-Muhtar, Chapter of *al-istinjā'*].

60 Slightly, in order for the impure water to spill off without spreading over his body [Maraqi al-Falah, page 29].

61 Also referred to as the "third finger."

62 This fear is extremely fanciful, so there is no need for such detail.

..........

..........

..........

..........

..........

..........

..........

..........

if he is not fasting. When he finishes, he washes his hand a second time and dries his bottom before standing if he is fasting[63].

63 This is out of fear that he may break his fast if water enters the anus and goes into the stomach, but it is highly improbable.

........................................................................................................

........................................................................................................

........................................................................................................

........................................................................................................

........................................................................................................

........................................................................................................

........................................................................................................

........................................................................................................

## Section of What al-Istinjā' is Permitted With

Exposing nakedness is not permitted for *al-istinjā'*, even if the impurity went past its orifice and the impurity that passed was in excess of the amount of the dirham. The prayer is not valid with it if there is something available to remove it. He should employ stratagems for its removal without exposure of nakedness in the presence of someone who can see him.

*Al-istinjā'* with bones, human or animal food, bricks, pottery, coal, glass, plaster, something of respect like a silk or cotton cloth, and the right hand is disliked[64] unless due to an excuse.

He enters the toilet with his left foot and seeks refuge with Allah from the accursed Satan before his entering. He sits supporting his weight on his left side and he does not speak unless it is for a necessity. Facing or turning one's back to the qiblah[65] is prohibitively disliked, even in buildings, and facing the direction of the sun or moon and the blowing of the wind. It is disliked that he urinates or defecates in water, shade[66], an animal den, the street, under a fruit-producing tree, and also urinating standing[67] unless due to an excuse.

---

64 Prohibitively disliked due to the hadith prohibiting using the right hand. See: [Al-Tirmidhi, 15].

65 Whilst relieving yourself [Maraqi al-Falah, page 33].

66 That people sit in [ibid.].

67 Mildly disliked due to the sound narrations of the Prophet ﷺ and a number of the companions (may Allah be pleased with them) standing and urinating. Imam al-Tahawi said, "There is no harm in urinating standing." [Al-Binayah Sharh al-Hidayah, Chapter of *al-istinjā'*, 1/172].

..........................................................................................

..........................................................................................

..........................................................................................

..........................................................................................

..........................................................................................

..........................................................................................

..........................................................................................

..........................................................................................

He exits the toilet with his right foot and says, “Praise is for Allah the one who removed harm from me and gave me well-being.”

................................................................................................................

................................................................................................................

................................................................................................................

................................................................................................................

................................................................................................................

................................................................................................................

................................................................................................................

................................................................................................................

## Section of the Rulings of Wudu

The pillars of wudu are four and they are its obligations:

1. *The first* is washing the face. Its limit vertically is from the beginning of the brow of the forehead to the bottom of the chin and its limit horizontally is what is between the two earlobes.
2. *The second* is washing his arms including his elbows.
3. *The third* is washing his feet including his ankles.
4. *The fourth* is wiping a quarter of his head.

Its cause is seeking to make permitted that which is not permitted except with it and this is its worldly ruling. Its other-worldly ruling is reward in the Hereafter.
Its condition of obligation is:

1. Intellect.
2. Puberty.
3. Islam.
4. The ability to use a sufficient amount of water.
5. The presence of legal impurity.
6. The absence of menstruation and postpartum bleeding (lochia).

................................................................................................

................................................................................................

................................................................................................

................................................................................................

................................................................................................

................................................................................................

................................................................................................

................................................................................................

7. The restriction of the time[68].

The condition of its validity is three:

1. Covering of the skin with purifying water.
2. Cessation of what negates it, like menstruation, postpartum bleeding, and legal impurity.
3. Disappearance of what prevents the reaching of water to the body like wax and fat.

68 When the time is not restricted, performing wudu is not obligatory immediately due to the fact that a person can pray at the beginning or end of the prayer time. However, if the time becomes restricted a person must perform wudu and pray.

........................................................................................................................

........................................................................................................................

........................................................................................................................

........................................................................................................................

........................................................................................................................

........................................................................................................................

........................................................................................................................

........................................................................................................................

## Section of Completion of the Rulings of Wudu

It is obligatory to wash the outer of a thick beard according to the most correct of that with which fatwa is given. Making the water reach the skin of a thin beard is obligatory. However, making the water reach the hair hanging from the circumference of the face is not obligatory, nor that which is covered by the lips when they are sealed. If fingers are closed together, a nail grows and covers the fingertip, or there is something in it[69] that blocks the water like dough then it is obligatory to wash what is under it. Filth, flea excrement and what is similar to it does not prevent. Moving a tight ring is obligatory.

If washing cuts on his feet harms him, then it is permitted to pass water over medicine that he placed on them. Washing is not repeated, nor wiping, over a place of hair after it being shaved, nor is washing repeated due to cutting his nails and moustache.

---

69 The fingernail.

## Section of the Sunnahs of Wudu

Eighteen things are sunnah in wudu:

1. Washing the hands to the wrists and,
2. mentioning Allah's name (*al-tasmiyah*) initially.
3. Cleaning the teeth with a brush in its beginning[70], even with a finger when it is not found.
4. Rinsing the mouth three times even with one scoop of water.
5. Rinsing the nose with three scoops of water.
6. Exaggerating in rinsing the mouth[71] and nose[72] for someone who is not fasting.
7. Running the fingers through a thick beard from the bottom of it with a handful of water.
8. Running fingers through the fingers and toes.
9. Washing three times.
10. Encompassing the head with wiping once.

---

70 Beginning with it at the time of rinsing the mouth is also sunnah according to the majority and others said it is before wudu [Maraqi al-Falah, page 41].

71 So that water reaches the top of the throat [Maraqi al-Falah, page 43].

72 So that water reaches above the soft gristle [ibid.].

........................................................................................................

........................................................................................................

........................................................................................................

........................................................................................................

........................................................................................................

........................................................................................................

........................................................................................................

........................................................................................................

11. Wiping the ears even with the water of the head.
12. Rubbing.
13. Continuity.
14. Intention.
15. Order as Allah (exalted is He) mentioned in His book.
16. Beginning with the right-hand sides,
17. the tips of the toes and fingers, and the front of the head.
18. Wiping the back of the neck, not the front[73].

It was said that the last four are recommended[74].

73 This is an innovation [Maraqi al-Falah, page 45].

74 This is the correct position in the school.

## Section of the Etiquettes[75] of Wudu

Fourteen things are from the etiquettes of wudu:

1. Sitting at a high place.
2. Facing the qiblah.
3. Not seeking assistance from someone else.
4. Not speaking with the general speech of people.
5. Joining between the intention of the heart and the action of the tongue.[76]
6. Supplication with the transmitted[77].
7. The mentioning of Allah's name with every limb.
8. Entering his little finger into earholes.
9. Moving his loose ring.
10. The rinsing of the mouth and nose with the right hand and clearing the nasal mucus with the left.

---

75 This comes under the scope of recommended actions but not sunnah.

76 i.e. verbalising the intention in order to solidify it.

77 Some supplications have been transmitted from the righteous; see the works of Imam al-Ghazali or other books for further details. In any case, a person can supplicate with any wording that is appropriate for the act of wudu.

........................................................................................................

........................................................................................................

........................................................................................................

........................................................................................................

........................................................................................................

........................................................................................................

........................................................................................................

........................................................................................................

11. Performing wudu before the entering of the time for someone who is not "excused."

12. Performing the two testimonies after it[78].

13. That he drinks from the remainder of the water used for wudu standing[79].

14. That he says, "*allāhummaj-ʿalnī minat-tawwābīn waj-ʿalnī minal mutaṭahhirīn*"[80]

---

78 The Prophet ﷺ said, "There isn't a single one of you who performs wudu and completes his wudu then says 'I testify that there is no god except Allah and I testify that Muhammad is His servant and His messenger' except that the eight doors of Heaven are opened for him, he may enter through any of them he wishes." [Muslim, 552] and [Abu Dawud, 169].

79 In accordance with the action of the Messenger of Allah ﷺ see: [Al-Bukhari, 1556] and [Muslim, 525].

80 Oh Allah make me from the constantly repentant and make me from those who purify themselves. See: [Quran 2:222].

## Section of Disliked Actions

Six things are disliked for the person making wudu:

1. Extravagance with water.
2. Stinginess with it.
3. Smacking the face with it.
4. Speaking with the general speech of people.
5. Seeking assistance from someone else[81].
6. Wiping the head three times with fresh water[82].

---

81 It was narrated from Imam al-Wabari that there is no harm in it because the servant of the Prophet ﷺ used to pour water over him [Maraqi al-Falah, page 49]. This is the sounder position and has been narrated in the sound hadith, see: [Muslim, 628, Chapter of Wiping Over the *Khuffayn]* and [Al-Bukhari, 363].

82 Because it turns into washing. However, if it is with the same water then there is no harm in it. See: [Radd al-Muhtar, Chapter of the Sunnahs of Wudu].

............................................................

............................................................

............................................................

............................................................

............................................................

............................................................

............................................................

............................................................

## Section of the Attributes[83] of Wudu

Wudu is of three categories:

1. The first is farḍ upon the one in minor legal impurity for prayer, even if it is additional (*nafl*). Also, for the funeral prayer, the prostration of recitation, and touching the Quran even if it is one verse[84].
2. The second is wājib[85] for circumambulation (*ṭawāf*) of the Kaaba.
3. The third is recommended for sleeping in purity[86], when waking from it, for continuity in wudu, for wudu over wudu, after backbiting, lying, slander, every wrong action, singing poetry[87], laughing out loud outside of prayer, washing a dead body and carrying it, for the time of every prayer, before the wash of major legal impurity, for someone in a state of major legal impurity when eating, drinking, sleeping, and having sexual intercourse, for anger, for Quran, Hadith, and narration of it[88], study of sacred knowledge, an adhan, an iqamah, a sermon, visiting the Prophet ﷺ, stopping

83 Meaning the legal rulings of wudu.

84 Even if it is in a different language [Maraqi al-Falah, page 50].

85 Not *farḍ* [See introduction]. Thus the circumambulation is valid but prohibitively disliked.

86 Due to the hadith: "When you take your place of rest then make wudu like your wudu for prayer then lie on your right-hand side" [Muslim, 6820].

87 Explicit worded poetry.

88 Hadith.

........................................................................................................

........................................................................................................

........................................................................................................

........................................................................................................

........................................................................................................

........................................................................................................

........................................................................................................

........................................................................................................

at Arafah, for going between *al-Ṣafā* and *al-Marwah*, eating camel meat[89], and for egression from disagreement of the ulama such as when he touches a woman[90].

89 Out of precaution due to it being an invalidator of wudu in the Hanbali School.

90 This invalidates wudu in the Shafi'i School. Likewise, a woman touching a man if they are both adults and not close-relatives and no barrier was between the touching.

## Section of the Invalidators of Wudu

Twelve things invalidate wudu:

1. What[91] exits from the two passages[92] except for wind from the front according to the soundest opinion[93].
2. Childbirth without seeing blood invalidates it.
3. Flowing impurity from other than those two[94] like blood and pus.
4. Vomiting food, water, a bloodclot, or bile if it fills the mouth. It[95] is what the mouth cannot close over except with constraint, according to the soundest opinion[96]. Separated vomit is added together if the cause is one[97].

---

91 Whether it is pure or impure, normal or abnormal, small or large. Therefore, the discharge from a woman's vagina even though considered pure with Abu Hanifah would invalidate wudu so don't be deluded by what is mentioned in some contemporary books about it not invalidating wudu because it has not been mentioned by any of the four schools. Despite this, moisture that may occur on the outer part of the vagina does not invalidate wudu, nor does a woman need to assume her wudu is broken until she is absolutely sure that a substance came out of the inner part of the vagina and appeared on the outer part.

92 Front or back.

93 A weaker opinion says wind from the front passage invalidates wudu.

94 Front or back passages [Maraqi al-Falah, page 53].

95 The amount of filling the mouth [Maraqi al-Falah, page 54].

96 A weaker position says it is what prevents speech [ibid.].

97 This is the position of Imam Muhammad bin al-Hasan and it is the sounder opinion [ibid.].

........................................................................................................

........................................................................................................

........................................................................................................

........................................................................................................

........................................................................................................

........................................................................................................

........................................................................................................

5. Blood that overpowered saliva or equalled it.

6. Sleep that the bottom wasn't fixed to the ground in.

7. Lifting of the bottom of a sleeping person before his waking even if he doesn't fall[98] according to the apparent opinion[99].

8. Unconsciousness.

9. Insanity.

10. Intoxication.

11. The laughing out loud of an adult who is awake in a prayer that has bowing and prostration, even if he intended by it exiting of the prayer[100].

12. Touching a vagina[101] with an erect penis without a barrier[102].

---

98 To the ground [Maraqi al-Falah, page 55].

99 Of the school [ibid.]. Thus, if he wakes every time he falls, then it does not invalidate wudu [Hashiyah al-Tahtawi, page 137]

100 A *mursal* narration mentions that some people laughed during the prayer and the Prophet ﷺ commanded them to repeat their wudu and their prayer. [Al-Tabarani, Al-Mu'jam al-Kabir, 1767] and [Al-Hathyami, Majma' al-Zawa'id, 2472]. This type of narration is considered as a proof with most jurists.

101 Or anus [Maraqi al-Falah, page 56].

102 That prevents the heat of the body [ibid.]. Imam Muhammad is of the stance that it does not invalidate which is based on *qiyas* (analogy) due to no fluid exiting, whereas Abu Hanifah and Abu Yusuf said that most of the time some fluid will exit, therefore, it will invalidate wudu on every occasion as a matter of precaution in acts of worship and their stance is *istiḥsān* [Hashiyah al-Tahtawi, page 139].

....................................................................................................

....................................................................................................

....................................................................................................

....................................................................................................

....................................................................................................

....................................................................................................

....................................................................................................

## Section of Ten Things That do not Invalidate Wudu

Ten things that do not invalidate wudu:

1. The appearance of blood that does not flow from its place.
2. The falling of flesh without the flowing of blood like warts (*al-ᶜirq al-madani*) that is called *rishtah*[103].
3. The exiting of a worm from a wound, ear, and nose.
4. Touching the penis[104].
5. Touching a woman.
6. Vomiting that does not fill the mouth.
7. Vomiting phlegm, even if it is a lot.
8. The swaying of a sleeping person in which the moving of his bottom was possible[105].
9. The sleep of a person firmly attached, even if he was leaning against something if it was removed then he would have fallen over according to the apparent stance[106], in both scenarios.

---

103 In Persian. The Dracunculus or Guinea worm (*Filaria medinensis*) see: Steingass's Persian dictionary.

104 Or the anus or backside, whether done with sexual desire or not [Maraqi al-Falah, page 57].

105 His bottom must have lifted off the ground with certainty for his wudu to be invalid due to the juristic principle "certainty is not removed with doubt."

106 Of the Hanafi School.

.......................................................................................................

.......................................................................................................

.......................................................................................................

.......................................................................................................

.......................................................................................................

.......................................................................................................

.......................................................................................................

10. The sleep of a person praying (even if he is bowing or prostrating) in the sunnah method[107].

Allah is the granter of success.

107 If he is not in a Sunnah posture, e.g. arms spread out and off the ground, then the wudu is invalid [Maraqi al-Falah, page 57].

.......................................................................................................................

.......................................................................................................................

.......................................................................................................................

.......................................................................................................................

.......................................................................................................................

.......................................................................................................................

.......................................................................................................................

## Section of What Necessitates Bathing

*Ghusl* (complete washing of the body) is obligatory from one of seven things:

1. The exiting of semen to the outer part of the body when it separates from its resting place with sexual desire without sexual intercourse.
2. The disapppearance of the head (glans) of the penis or its amount from what is cut off from it[108] in one of the two passages of a live human being.
3. The ejaculation of semen due to coitus with a dead woman or animal.
4. The presence of a fine liquid after sleep if his penis was not erect before sleeping.
5. The presence of wetness that he believes to be semen after his waking from intoxication and unconsciousness.
6. Menstruation and postpartum bleeding[109].

Even if these things occurred before Islam according to the soundest opinion.

7. It is obligatory to wash the deceased as a communal obligation.

108 If the glans has been cut off.

109 When it ends [Maraqi al-Falah, page 61].

..........................................................................................

..........................................................................................

..........................................................................................

..........................................................................................

..........................................................................................

..........................................................................................

## Section of Ten Things That Bathing is Not Required From

There are ten things that bathing is not required from:

1. Pre-ejaculate[110].
2. Prostatic fluid.
3. A wet-dream without any wetness.
4. Childbirth without seeing blood after it according to the correct opinion[111].
5. Penetration with a cloth preventing the presence of sexual pleasure.
6. An enema[112].
7. The inserting of a finger or something similar[113] into one of the two passages.
8. Coitus with an animal,
9. or a dead woman without ejaculation.
10. Penetration of a virgin girl whose hymen remains intact without ejaculation.

---

110 Also known as pre-ejaculatory fluid, preseminal fluid, or Cowper's fluid, and colloquially as pre-cum. It is a clear, colourless, viscous fluid that is emitted from the urethra of the penis during sexual arousal.

111 This is the opinion of Abu Yusuf and Muhammad. Abu Hanifah says that she makes ghusl out of precaution [Maraqi al-Falah, page 62].

112 Administration of medicine into the rectum.

113 Like a synthetic penis made from leather [Maraqi al-Falah, page 62].

............................................................................................................

............................................................................................................

............................................................................................................

............................................................................................................

............................................................................................................

............................................................................................................

### Section for Clarifying the Obligatory Parts of Ghusl

Eleven things are obligatory in bathing:

1. Washing the mouth,
2. nose,
3. and the body once.
4. The inside of the foreskin that there is no difficulty in pulling back.
5. The navel.
6. A hole that is not enclosed.
7. The inside of a plait from the hair of a man, not a plait from the hair of a woman if the water flows to its roots.
8. The skin of the beard.
9. The skin of the moustache,
10. and the eyebrow.
11. The outer vagina.

.....................................................................................................

.....................................................................................................

.....................................................................................................

.....................................................................................................

.....................................................................................................

.....................................................................................................

## Section of the Sunnahs of Bathing

Twelve things are sunnah in bathing:

1. Beginning with mentioning Allah's name (*al-tasmiyah*),
2. intention,
3. and washing the hands up to the wrists.
4. Washing an impurity if it is on its own.
5. Washing his private parts.
6. Then he performs wudu like his wudu for prayer, thus he washes three times and wipes the head
7. but he delays washing his feet if he is standing in a place where the water gathers.
8. Then he pours the water over his body his body thrice and if he submerged himself in running water or that which has its ruling and he remained in it[114] he has completed the sunnah.
9. He begins with his head when he is pouring the water
10. and washes his right shoulder after it then his left shoulder.
11. He rubs his body.
12. He makes his washing continuous[115].

---

114 For the length of time that it takes to perform wudu and ghusl [Maraqi al-Falah, page 66].

115 Without interruption.

........................................................................................................

........................................................................................................

........................................................................................................

........................................................................................................

........................................................................................................

........................................................................................................

## Section of the Etiquettes of Bathing and its Disliked Actions

The etiquettes of bathing are the etiquettes of wudu except that he does not face the qiblah because it will most likely be with exposure of nakedness. What is disliked in it is that which is disliked in wudu.

## Section of the Sunnahs and Recommended Actions of Bathing

Bathing is sunnah for four things:

1. The Friday prayer.
2. The two Eid prayers.
3. For *iḥrām*[116].
4. For the hajj pilgrim on Arafah after al-zawwāl (the moving of the sun from its zenith).

Bathing is recommended for sixteen things:

1. The one who converts to Islam in a pure state.
2. The one who reaches puberty by age[117].
3. The one who comes to his senses from insanity.
4. From cupping.
5. Washing a dead body.

---

116 Entering the state of ritual consecration for a pilgrim performing hajj or umrah.
117 If no signs of puberty appear before this age then the fatwa-given opinion is that this is with the completion of 15 lunar years for a boy and a girl (5315.55 days/14.55 solar years). [Maraqi al-Falah, page 69].

6. The Night of Exemption[118].
7. The Night of Decree (*Laylatul-Qadr*) if he sees it.
8. For entering the city of the Prophet ﷺ.
9. For stopping at Muzdalifah the morning of the day of *al-Naḥr*[119].
10. At the time of entering Mecca.
11. For the *ṭawāf* (circumambulation) of visiting[120].
12. For the eclipse prayer.
13. Asking for rain.
14. Fear.
15. Darkness[121].
16. A strong wind.

---

118 The 15th Sha'ban [Maraqi al-Falah, page 69]. It has been narrated that the Messenger of Allah ﷺ said, "Indeed Allah surely looks on the night of the fifteenth of Sha'ban then forgives all of His creation except a polytheist or a schismatic hate-monger" [Ibn Majah (1390), Al-Bayhaqi –Shu'ab al-Iman (3833), Ibn Hibban (5665), Al-Tabarani – Al-Awsat (6772), Ahmad (6642)]. Albani said: "Sahih with all of its chains" [Al-Silsilah al-Sahihah 218/3 no. 1144] Ahmad Shakir said: "Sahih with all of its chains" in his commentary on the Musnad of Imam Ahmad. Husayn al-Darani said: "The ahadith are individually weak but sahih with all of their chains" in his footnotes on Majma' al-Zawa'id [190/17].

119 10th Dhul Hijjah. The time of stopping is after al-Fajr, even if for a brief moment, in the Hanafi School [Maraqi al-Falah, page 69].

120 The obligatory tawaf of hajj.

121 That occurs during the day [Maraqi al-Falah, page 69].

..........

..........

..........

..........

..........

..........

..........

..........

## Section of Tayammum

It is valid with eight conditions:

1. The first is intention and the reality of it is the determination of the heart to perform the action. The time of it is when striking the hand on that which tayammum is being performed with. The conditions of the validity of the intention[122] are three:

    a. Islam.

    b. Discernment[123].

    c. Knowledge of what he is intending.

It is a condition for the validity of the intention of tayammum for the prayer[124] one of three things, either:

a. Intention of purification or,

b. making the prayer permitted or,

---

122 In general.

123 This excludes an insane person and a child under the age of discernment, roughly 6 or 7 years old, e.g. when they are old enough to discern different monetary coins or the difference between a donkey and a horse.

124 Specifically.

........................................................................................................

........................................................................................................

........................................................................................................

........................................................................................................

........................................................................................................

........................................................................................................

........................................................................................................

........................................................................................................

c. intention of an intended act of worship that is not valid without purification.

Therefore, he doesn't pray with it if he intended tayammum alone[125] or he intended it for reciting the Quran and he is not in a state of major legal impurity.

2. The second one is an excuse permitting tayammum. Like his being a mile's[126] distance from water even if he is in the city, the occurrence of illness, cold that from it perishing or illness is feared, fear of an enemy, severe thirst[127], a need for making dough not cooking soup, loss of a tool[128], fear of missing the funeral or Eid prayer even when building[129]. Fear of the Friday prayer and prayer of the time is not an excuse.

3. The third one is that the tayammum is with a something pure from the category of the earth like dust, stones, and sand not wood, silver, and gold.

4. The fourth one is covering the area with wiping.

5. The fifth is that he wipes with the entire hand or the majority of it[130]

---

125 Just for the sake of performing tayammum.

126 One third of a *farsakh* which is approximately 1.86km, not the UK mile which is 1.6km.

127 For himself or his animal, even if it is a dog [Maraqi al-Falah, page 73].

128 Like a rope or bucket if using a well [Maraqi al-Falah, page 73].

129 Upon them if in the prayer and overcome by something breaking one's wudu. If so, tayammum can be made and the prayer can be continued. However, tayammum is restricted to the Eid and funeral prayers.

130 Or anything that takes its place [Maraqi al-Falah, page 75]. This condition is debatable due to what is mentioned in *Al-Aṣl* and elsewhere that if a person where to roll around in the dirt or dust with the intention of tayammum then it suffices

inasmuch as that if he wiped with two fingers it is not permitted even if he repeats it until it covers as opposed to wiping the head.

6. The sixth one is that it is with two strikes with the inner part of the hands even if it is in one place. His body being hit by dust will take the place of the two strikes if he wipes it[131] with the intention of tayammum.
7. The seventh is the cessation of what negates it from menstruation, postpartum bleeding, or legal impurity.
8. The eighth is the disappearance of what prevents wiping like wax and fat.

Its cause and conditions of being obligatory are as was mentioned in wudu. Its two pillars are:

1. Wiping the arms
2. and face.

The sunnahs of tayammum are seven:

1. Mentioning Allah's name in the beginning.
2. The order.
3. Continuity.
4. Bringing forward the hands after placing them in the dust,

---

[Al-Aṣl *aka* Al-Mabsut, Al-Muhit al-Burhani, Al-Tatarkhaniyyah all in the Chapters of Tayammum]. This is also mentioned in the hadith of Ammar bin Yasir (may Allah be pleased with him), see: [Al-Bukhari, 338].

131 See previous footnote.

5. pushing them away,
6. shaking them, and
7. spreading the fingers.

The delaying of tayammum is recommended for the one who hopes for water before the exiting of the time[132]. Delaying is obligatory with a promise of water[133], even if he fears making up the prayer. Delaying is also obligatory with a promise of a garment[134] or a waterskin as long as he does not fear making up the prayer. Seeking water up to the distance of 400 paces is obligatory if he believes it to be close with safety and if not, then no[135]. Requesting it is obligatory from whoever is with him if he is in a place where people are not stingy and if he is not given it except for the standard price then he must buy it for that price if it[136] is surplus to his maintenance. He prays with one tayammum whatever he wishes from the obligatory and voluntary prayers. Performance of it before the time is valid. If the majority of the body or half of it is wounded, he makes tayammum. If the majority of it is healthy, he washes it and wipes the wounded part but he does not join between washing and tayammum. The invalidator of wudu invalidates it and the ability of usage of a sufficient amount of water[137]. As for the one whose arms and feet are amputated, if his face has wounding in it, then he prays without purification and he does not repeat.

---

132 The recommended time [Maraqi al-Falah, page 77].
133 If the water is present or close by [Maraqi al-Falah, page 77].
134 For a naked person.
135 The sounder position is what has been mentioned in *Bada'i al-Sana'i* that it is obligatory as long as there is no harm to himself and his travelling companions with waiting. See: [Hashiyah al-Tahtawi and Bada'i al-Sana'i, Chapters of Tayammum].
136 The money or payment that he has.
137 Even if he is only able to wash once [Maraqi al-Falah, page 79].

..............................................................................................................

..............................................................................................................

..............................................................................................................

..............................................................................................................

..............................................................................................................

..............................................................................................................

## Section of Wiping over Leather Socks

Wiping over leather socks is valid for minor legal impurity for men and women even if they are made from something thick other than leather[138], whether they have a sole from leather or not. Seven conditions are stipulated for the permissibility of wiping over socks:

1. The first is wearing them after washing the feet even if before the completion of wudu if he completes it before the occurrence of an invalidator of wudu.
2. The second is their covering of the ankles.
3. The third is the ability of continuous walking in them. Thus, it is not permitted over a sock made from glass, wood, or iron.
4. The fourth is that each one is free from a hole the size of three of the smallest toes.
5. The fifth is their clinging on to the feet without fastening[139].
6. The sixth is their preventing the reaching of water to the body[140].
7. The seventh is that the amount of three of the smallest fingers are

---

138 Like wool, broadcloth, and thick cotton [Maraqi al-Falah, page 80].

139 An external fastening, as for one connected to the sock then it is valid. See: [Radd al-Muhtar, Chapter of Wiping Over Leather Socks].

140 Generally, when wiped over. However, they do not have to be 100% waterproof. In Al-Lubab fi Sharh al-Kitab in the Section of Wiping Over Socks, he mentions, "They prevent water reaching the feet when wiped over". However, in Majma' al-Fawa'id and Imdad al-Fattah, it mentions if one were to walk over wet ground in them.

remaining from the front of the foot[141]. Thus, if he is missing the front of his foot, he doesn't wipe over his leather sock even if the heel of the foot is present.

The resident person wipes for a day and night and the traveller for three days and three nights[142]. The beginning of the period is from the time of legal impurity after wearing the leather socks. If a resident person wiped and then travelled before the completion of the period, he completes the period of a traveller. If a traveller becomes resident after him wiping for a day and night, he removes them, and if not, he completes a day and night.

The obligatory wiping is the amount of three of the smallest fingers on the outer of the front of every foot.

Its sunnahs are spreading the fingers out wide from the tips of the toes to the shin.

Four things invalidate wiping of the leather socks:

1. Every thing that invalidates wudu.
2. Removing the leather sock, even with the exiting of the majority of the foot to the leg of the sock.
3. The contact of water in the leather sock with the majority of one of the feet according to the sound opinion.
4. The elapsing of the period if he does not fear losing his foot due to the cold.

After the last three, he only washes his feet.

Wiping is not permitted over a turban, hat, burqa, and gloves.

141 This is so that there is a place of wiping.
142 72 hours or 4320 minutes.

## Section of the Ruling of a Splint and Similar to it

If blood is drawn from a limb or it is cut or broken, then he ties it with a cloth or a splint and he is unable to wash the limb or unable to wipe it then wiping over the majority of what the limb has been tied with is wājib[143].

Wiping over what is apparent of the body between the bandage of the one whom blood has been drawn from[144] is sufficient.

Wiping is like washing so it is not limited to a time-period nor is tying the splint in a state of purity conditional and wiping the splint of one foot whilst washing the other is permitted. Wiping is not void due to it falling off before healing. It is permitted to replace it for another one but repetition of wiping over it is not required, but repetition of it is better.

If his eye becomes infected and he is ordered[145] not to wash his eye or his nail breaks and he places medicine, resin, or gallbladder skin on it and removing it harms him then wiping is permitted for him. If wiping harms him then he leaves it. Wiping over the leather sock[146], splint, and head does not require intention.

143 It has also been narrated that it is recommended and some said it is farḍ [Maraqi al-Falah, page 84].
144 And what is similar to it if undoing it harms him due to necessity so that the water does not flow to it and harm the wound, but if undoing it does not cause any harm then he undoes it, washes the healthy part, and wipes the wounded part, but if wiping harms him then he leaves it [Maraqi al-Falah, page 84].
145 By a professional Muslim doctor or he strongly believes that it will cause him harm [Maraqi al-Falah, page 85].
146 Or thick sock.

.......................................................................................................

.......................................................................................................

.......................................................................................................

.......................................................................................................

.......................................................................................................

.......................................................................................................

.......................................................................................................

## Section of Menstruation, Postpartum Bleeding, and Dysfunctional Uterine Bleeding

Menstruation, postpartum bleeding, and *Dysfunctional Uterine Bleeding* exit the vagina; thus, menstruation is blood that the womb of an adult woman pushes out not having any illness, pregnancy, and not having reached the age of menopause. The minimum menstruation is three days[147], its average is five, and its maximum is ten[148].

Postpartum bleeding is the blood after childbirth, its maximum is forty days and there is no limit to its minimum.

*DUB*[149] is blood that is less than three days and more than ten in relation to menstruation, and more than forty in relation to postpartum bleeding.

The minimum amount of purity separating between two menstruations is fifteen days and there is no maximum limit except for the one who reaches puberty with *DUB*[150].

Eight things are prohibited due to menstruation and postpartum bleeding:

1. The prayer.
2. Fasting.

---

147 72 hours.
148 240 hours.
149 Dysfunctional Uterine Bleeding.
150 In this scenario 10 days will be considered as menstruation and 20 days as purity until her habit bleeding becomes normal. See: [Al-Lubab fi Sharh al-Kitab, Chapter of Dysfunctional Uterine Bleeding].

.......................................................................................................
.......................................................................................................
.......................................................................................................
.......................................................................................................
.......................................................................................................
.......................................................................................................
.......................................................................................................

3. Recitation of a verse of the Quran[151],
4. and touching it except with a cover.
5. Entering the mosque.
6. *Al-Ṭawāf*[152].
7. Sexual intercourse.
8. Sexual enjoyment of what is below the navel to below the knee.

If the bleeding ceases due to the maximum menstruation and postpartum bleeding then coitus is permitted without ghusl. However, it is not permitted if it ceases due to the completion of her habit unless she performs ghusl, or makes tayammum and prays, or the prayer becomes a debt in her liability; this would be that she finds time, after the cessation from the time that the blood ceases, sufficient for ghusl and the *taḥrīmah* or more than these two but doesn't perform ghusl nor tayammum until the time exits.

The menstruating and postpartum woman makes up her fasting not the prayer.

Five things are prohibited with major legal impurity:

1. The prayer.
2. Recitation of a verse of Quran,
3. and touching it except with a cover.
4. Entering the mosque.
5. Al-Ṭawāf.

---

151 Except with the intention of dhikr (remembrance of Allah) [Maraqi al-Falah, page 88].
152 The anticlockwise circling of the Kaaba.

..........

..........

..........

..........

..........

..........

..........

Three things are prohibited for the one in a state of minor legal impurity:

1. The prayer.
2. Al-Ṭawāf.
3. Touching a copy of the Quran except with a cover.

The blood of DUB is like a constant nosebleed; it does not prevent prayer, fasting, or coitus. The woman with DUB and the one with an excuse like urine incontinence or loose bowels makes wudu for the time of every *farḍ*[153]. They can pray whatever they wish from the obligatory and voluntary prayers with it. The wudu of those with an excuse is invalid with the exiting of the time only. A person will not become one who has an excuse until the excuse covers him for a complete prayer time without any cessation for the amount of wudu and prayer and this is the condition of its establishment. The condition of its continuity is it being present in every prayer time after that even if once. The condition of its cessation and the exiting of the person from being excused is a complete prayer time being free of it.

153 The *time* of every obligatory prayer, not every obligatory prayer.

## Section of Impurities and Purification of Them

Impurity divides into two categories:

1. Severe and,
2. Light.

The severe is such as wine[154], flowing blood[155], carrion meat and its hide, the urine of inedible animals[156], dog excrement, the excrement of beasts of prey and their saliva, chicken, duck, and goose excrement, and whatever invalidates wudu with its exiting the body of a person[157].

The light is such as horse urine, likewise the urine of edible animals, and the faeces of inedible birds.

The amount of a dirham[158] is excused from the severe, and what is less than a quarter of a garment or body from the light.

---

154 Wine is raw grape juice when it is left to ferment, becomes intoxicating, and spits off froth [Maraqi al-Falah, page 94].

155 Not what remains in the lean meat and fat, nor what remains in the veins of a slaughtered animal, the blood of the liver, spleen, and heart, nor what does not invalidate wudu according to the sound opinion [Maraqi al-Falah, page 95].

156 Such as a human being (even if a breastfeeding baby) and a wolf [Maraqi al-Falah, page 95].

157 Such as flowing blood, semen, pre-ejaculate, prostatic fluid, DUB, menstruation, postpartum bleeding, a mouthful of vomit, and severe impurity [Maraqi al-Falah, page 95].

158 By weight in relation to solid impurity, which is 20 *qirāṭ*, and by surface in relation to liquid impurity which is the amount of the palm of the hand [Maraqi al-Falah, page 96]. It is approximately 4-4.5 grams in weight.

..........................................................................................................

..........................................................................................................

..........................................................................................................

..........................................................................................................

..........................................................................................................

..........................................................................................................

The spray of urine like the tips of needles is excused.

If an impure blanket or soil become moist from the sweat of a sleeping person or the wetness of a foot and the trace of the impurity appears on the body or the foot then they both become impure, and if not then no. Just as a dry pure garment will not become impure that is wrapped in a wet impure garment that the moisture does not drip out of if squeezed.

A wet garment will not become impure with its spreading on dry impure earth thus becoming moist from it, nor by wind that blew over an impurity and then came into contact with the garment unless a trace of it[159] appears on it[160].

Something that becomes impure by a visible impurity is purified by removal of its substance even if once[161] according to the sound opinion, and a trace whose removal is difficult does not harm. The invisible is removed by washing it thrice and squeezing after every time[162].

Impurity is purified from a garment and body with water and every removing liquid such as vinegar and rosewater. A leather sock and [163]what is analogous to it is purified from an impurity that has a body by rubbing, even if it is moist. A sword and what is analogous to it is purified by wiping.

When the trace of impurity disappears from the earth and it dries then prayer is valid on it but not tayammum from it, and what is with it of plants and existing grass becomes pure with its drying.

An impurity whose substance transforms becomes pure like when it becomes salt, or when it is scorched with fire[164].

---

159 The impurity.

160 The garment.

161 Repetition of washing is not conditional [Maraqi al-Falah, page 98].

162 Placing it in running water suffices washing thrice and squeezing [Maraqi al-Falah, page 99].

163 According to the chosen position for fatwa, and the majority of scholars hold this opinion [Maraqi al-Falah, page 100].

164 The ashes of faeces are not impure (otherwise it necessitates the impurity of

.................................................................................................................................

.................................................................................................................................

.................................................................................................................................

.................................................................................................................................

.................................................................................................................................

Dry semen becomes pure by the scraping of it off a garment and the body and the moist[165] becomes pure by the washing of it.

---

bread in every land) and salt that was a donkey or a pig, or faeces that fell into a well and became clay is not impure [Al-Durr al-Mukhtar, Chapter of Impurities].

Know that the legal reason with Muhammad is change and the alteration of reality and fatwa is given on it due to affliction as is known from what passed. The necessary consequence of it is that ruling not being restricted to soap, thus everything which has change and an alteration of reality and there is widespread affliction regarding it will enter it. So, it is said, "Likewise for cooked syrup if its raisins are made impure especially that mice enter it, urinate and defecate in it, and possibly die in it." Likewise, one of my teachers researched and said, "Based on this, if sesame seeds become impure and then become paste they become pure, especially when the tribulation is widespread with it" and he made analogy to it based on when a sparrow falls into a well until it becomes mud, its removal is not binding due to transformation. I say, but it may be said that there is no alteration of reality in the syrup because it is juice that has solidified by cooking, similarly sesame seeds if they are thrashed and its oil is mixed with its particles, in this there is only a change of a description such as milk turning into cheese, wheat turning into flour, and flour turning into bread. As opposed to the likeness of wine turning into vinegar, a donkey falling into a salt refinery and turning into salt, likewise, the dregs of wine turning into tartar (wine stone/potassium bitartrate), and faeces turning into ash or clay, because in all of that there is alteration of reality to another reality not just the alteration of a description (as will come) and Allah knows best [Radd al-Muhtar, Chapter of Impurities].

The aspect of the position of Muhammad is that when impurity transforms and its descriptions and meanings change it desists from being an impurity because it is a name for a described essence, thus it becomes absent with the absence of the description and becomes like wine when it becomes vinegar [Bada'i al-Sana'i, Chapter of Impurities, 1:85].

165 Semen.

.......................................................................................................................

.......................................................................................................................

.......................................................................................................................

.......................................................................................................................

.......................................................................................................................

## Section of Purification of Skins of Dead Animals and Similar to it

Dead animal skin becomes pure by literal tanning like pods of the gum arabic[166] tree, and by legal tanning like covering with earth and drying in the sun except for pigskin and human skin.

Legal slaughter purifies the skin of an inedible animal but not its meat according to the most correct of that with which fatwa is given[167].

Every thing that blood does not flow through does not become impure with death such as hair, cut feathers[168], the horn, the hoof, and the bone as long as there is no marrow in it[169]. The nerves are impure according to the sound opinion.

The musk pod is pure like musk and the consumption of it is halal. Civet[170] is pure; the prayer of a person fragranced with it is valid.

---

166 *Acacia nilotica.*

167 Of two conflicting verified opinions concerning the purity of the meat of an inedible animal [Maraqi al-Falah, page 103].

168 Because the root of the plucked is impure [Maraqi al-Falah, page 103].

169 The bone [Maraqi al-Falah, page 103].

170 A fluid secreted from the anus of a civet cat used as a fragrance.

........................................................................................................

........................................................................................................

........................................................................................................

........................................................................................................

........................................................................................................

........................................................................................................

........................................................................................................

........................................................................................................

# The Book of Prayer

Three things are conditional for its obligation:

1. Islam.
2. Puberty.
3. Intellect.

Children are commanded with it at seven years[171] and smacked for it at ten with a hand, not a piece of wood[172].

Its causes are its times[173] and it is obligatory at the beginning of the time as an expanded obligation. The prayer times are five:

---

171 Lunar years.

172 As a deterrent, according to what he can bear, and it must not be more than three strikes with his hand [Maraqi al-Falah, page 105]. Also, the face and head must be avoided as well as bruising, marking, or harm.

173 Inasmuch as that if one were to pray al-Ẓuhr, for example, and travel back into the prayer time so that it enters again, then the obligation to pray al-Ẓuhr is repeated. For a more detailed discussion see: [Radd al-Muhtar, Case of if the Sun Returns After Its Setting, Section of Prayer Times].

........................................................................................................

........................................................................................................

........................................................................................................

........................................................................................................

........................................................................................................

........................................................................................................

........................................................................................................

........................................................................................................

1. (*Al-Fajr*)[174] Dawn time from the appearance of true dawn[175] until just before sunrise.

2. (*Al-Ẓuhr*) Noon time from the movement of the sun[176] until the

---

174 Two opinions are mentioned regarding the beginning of true dawn. It is mentioned in Al-Muhit al-Burhani, "The time of fasting is from the rising of the second dawn which is the dawn twilight that spreads and scatters in the horizon until the time of the setting of the sun, the exiting of the time of fasting. It was not transmitted from them whether consideration is with the first rising of the second dawn or its spreading and scattering and the scholars differed regarding it, some of them said consideration is with the its first rising and some of them said consideration is with its spreading. The Shaykh and Imam Shams al-A'immah al-Hulwani (may Allah have mercy upon him) said, 'The first opinion is safer and the second is more accommodating.'" [Al-Muhit al-Burhani, Book of Fasting].

According to my own observations the initial light of dawn occurs around -16° of the sun's depression below the horizon. The time of spreading across the horizon and edges of the sky is observed around and later than -12° of the sun's depression below the horizon, this occurs all year round for most of the UK (excluding some parts of Scotland).

175 As opposed to false dawn which is termed as zodiacal light. Ibn Abidin mentions, "The thing considered for true dawn is the dawn twilight that spreads on the horizon i.e. that whose light spreads in the edges of the sky… The Shaykh Khalil al-Kamili mentioned in his supercommentary on the treatise of the Astrolabe that the variance between the two dawns, likewise, between the red twilight and the white twilight is by 3°." [Radd al-Muhtar, The Book of Prayer]. It may be that the degrees mentioned here are the degrees of the azimuth which are approximately the same as the degrees of the sun's altitude in Syria for the phenomena of the two twilights. Allah knows best.

176 From the middle of the sky (i.e. solar noon) [Maraqi al-Falah, page 105]. The movement of the sun is known as *zawāl* in Arabic. In Al-Muhit al-Burhani it mentions, "If you want to know the movement of the sun, then what is transmitted from Abu Hanifah is that he looks at the disc of the sun and as long as it remains in the middle of the sky, then it has not moved. When it descends slightly, it has moved."

shadow of everything is double its length or equal to it excluding the zenith[177] shadow[178], al-Ṭaḥāwi[179] chose the second opinion and it is the opinion of the two companions[180].

3. (*Al-ᶜAṣr*) Mid-Afternoon time from the beginning of the increase of more than equal length or double length until the setting of the sun.

4. (*Al-Maghrib*) Sunset time is from it until the setting of the red twilight according to the fatwa-given opinion[181].

5. (*Al-ᶜIshā'*) Night prayer and *al-Witr* are from it until dawn.

Al-Witr is not done before the night prayer due to the necessary order and whoever does not experience their time[182] then they are not obligatory for him[183].

---

[Al-Muhit al-Burhani, Chapter of the Prayer Times].

177 The highest point of the sun in the sky. This always occurs when the sun is at an azimuth of 180° in the exact direction of south.

178 Which is excluded from the total time.

179 Imam Abu Ja'far Ahmad bin Muhammad al-Tahawi (321 AH/933 CE).

180 Abu Yusuf and Muhammad (may Allah have mercy upon them).

181 It is a narration from the Imam (Abu Hanifah) and fatwa is given on it, and they both (Abu Yusuf and Muhammad) held this opinion [Maraqi al-Falah, page 106]. One should note that this still occurs all year round in most of the UK (excluding parts of Scotland) based on the globally agreed-upon view that the red twilight disappears at roughly -12.5° depression. Also, the difference between the red and white twilight is alleged to have a difference of 3°.

182 The night prayer (*al-ᶜIshā'*) and al-Witr [Maraqi al-Falah, page 107].

183 This is an opinion formed and chosen by later scholars such as al-Hulwani, al-Nasafi, al-Haskafi and others. Other ulama such as Ibn al-Humam, al-Zayla'i, al-Marjani and the Shafi'i School held the opinion that the prayer time should be

Two obligatory prayers are not joined in one time because of an excuse except at Arafah for the hajj pilgrim with the condition of the highest leader[184] and *al-iḥrām*[185]. Thus al-Ẓuhr and al-ʿAṣr are combined a prior combining[186], al-Maghrib and al-ʿIshā' are combined at Muzdalifah and al-Maghrib is not valid on the way to Muzdalifah.

---

estimated. A number of ways have been discussed by contemporary ulama on how this should be done including dividing the night into halves, dividing the night into thirds, applying the mean fractions of the prayer times throughout the year, applying the fractions of the prayer times at night from the closest area, following the last time when prayer times were normal, joining between al-Maghrib al-ʿIshā', and making up al-ʿIshā' as a missed prayer. [See *Shedding The Light On The Dawn* by Dr. A. Yusuf for a more comprehensive discussion]. I would suggest dividing the time between sunset and sunrise into thirds, making the first third for the time of al-Maghrib, the second for the time of al-ʿIshā', and the third for the time of al-Fajr for the following reasons:

1. There are three prayers to consider with their relevant times, so logically, dividing the night into three parts makes sense.
2. The night being divided into thirds is mentioned frequently in the Quran and the Hadith in relation to the prayer. Also, in areas of than the prayer such as bequests, etiquettes of eating etc. a third has been considered as a maximum limit.
3. It is a more natural and simpler way of estimation for the layperson.
4. There is no dependency on angles of the sun's depression or complex scientific data, so it can be applied universally in any area where the sun sets and rises.

184 Meaning the head of state or his deputy [Maraqi al-Falah, page 108].
185 A state of sanctity that the pilgrim goes into when performing a minor or major pilgrimage.
186 In the time of al-Ẓuhr.

Brightening[187] is recommended for al-Fajr for men. Cooling[188] is recommended for al-Ẓuhr in the summer and hastening it in the winter unless on a cloudy day, hence it is delayed on it. Delaying al-ʿAṣr is recommended as long as the sun has not changed and hastening it on a cloudy day. Hastening al-Maghrib is recommended unless on a cloudy day, hence it is delayed on it. Delaying al-ʿIshā' until a third of the night is recommended and hastening it in cloudiness. Delaying al-Witr until the end of the night is recommended for the one who is confident of waking up[189].

187 Delaying in order to illuminate [Maraqi al-Falah, page 108].
188 Delaying the prayer until the cooler time.
189 If not then he prays al-Witr before sleep [Maraqi al-Falah, page 111].

........................................................................................................

........................................................................................................

........................................................................................................

........................................................................................................

........................................................................................................

........................................................................................................

........................................................................................................

........................................................................................................

## Section of Disliked Times

There are three times that nothing of the *faraᶜiḍ*[190] and the *wājibāt*[191] that became binding before their[192] entering are valid in:

1. At the rising of the sun until it has fully elevated[193].
2. At the time of the sun's zenith until it passes[194].
3. At the sun's yellowing[195] until it sets.

The performance of what became compulsory in them[196] is valid with dislike such as a funeral prayer that became present and the prostration of a verse that was recited in them[197] just as the ᶜaṣr prayer of that day is valid at the setting of the sun with dislike. Voluntary prayer is disliked in these three times, a dislike of prohibition, even if it has a cause such as a vow or two units of prayer for ṭawāf.

190 Plural of farḍ.
191 Plural of wājib.
192 The disliked times [Maraqi al-Falah, page 112].
193 And becomes white, the amount of a spear or two spears [Maraqi al-Falah, page 112]. This equates to at least a 4.5° altitude but needs investigating.
194 Meaning it inclines towards the direction of the west [Maraqi al-Falah, page 112]. This is a brief amount of time possibly a minute or two. However, further observations need to be conducted to determine this.
195 And weakening until the eye is able to face it [Maraqi al-Falah, page 112]. This occurs at a 4.5° altitude of the sun.
196 The three times [Maraqi al-Falah, page 113].
197 And a voluntary prayer that he began in them [Maraqi al-Falah, page 113].

Voluntary prayer after the onset of al-Fajr with more than its sunnah is disliked and after its prayer[198], after the prayer of al-ᶜAṣr, before the prayer of al-Maghrib, at the coming out of the imam to give a sermon until he finishes the prayer, at the time of the *iqāmah* except for the sunnahs of al-Fajr, before the Eid prayer even at home, after it in the mosque, between the two joinings at Arafah and Muzdalifah, when there is constriction of the obligatory prayer time, repressing the two filths[199], in the presence of food that one's self craves, and anything that busies the mind and ruins humility.

---

198 Obligatory dawn prayer [Maraqi al-Falah, page 113].
199 Urine and faeces, likewise, wind [Maraqi al-Falah, page 114].

## Section of the Adhan

The adhan and the *iqāmah* are an emphasised sunnah for the obligatory prayers for men and they are both disliked for women, even if one prays alone; whether immediately performed, made up, travelling, or resident.

One says "*Allāhu akbar*" four times at its beginning and says "*Allāhu akbar*" twice at the end like the rest of its wordings. There is no reiteration in the two testimonies. The iqāmah is like it and he adds after "*falāḥ*" of al-Fajr "*aṣ-ṣalātu khayrun min an-nawm*[200]" twice and after "falāḥ" of the iqāmah "*qad qāmatiṣ-ṣālah.*[201]" He takes his time in the adhan and hastens in the iqāmah. It is not sufficient in Persian[202] even if it is known that it is the adhan according to the stronger view.

It is recommended that the caller to prayer is righteous, knowledgeable of the sunnah[203] and the prayer times, in a state of wudu, and facing the qiblah unless he is riding. He places his fingers in his ears, turns his face to the right with "*al-ṣalāh*" and to the left with "*al-falāḥ*", and rotates in his minaret. He separates between the adhan and the iqāmah enough that the regular adherers of the prayer will attend with consideration of the recommended time and in al-Maghrib with a short pause enough for the recital of three short verses or three steps. He summons again after the adhan like his saying "Adhere to the prayer! Adhere to the prayer oh worshippers!"

---

200 The prayer is better than sleep.
201 The prayer has been established.
202 What is intended is other than Arabic [Maraqi al-Falah, page 117].
203 In relation to the adhan [Maraqi al-Falah, page 117].

........................................................................................................

........................................................................................................

........................................................................................................

........................................................................................................

........................................................................................................

........................................................................................................

........................................................................................................

........................................................................................................

Singing and mispronouncing is disliked. Also disliked is the iqāmah and the adhan of a person in a state of minor legal impurity, the adhan of a person in a state of major legal impurity, a child who doesn't comprehend, an insane person, an intoxicated person, a woman, a sinner, a person sat down, and speech in between the adhan and the iqāmah. It is recommended to repeat it[204] but not the iqāmah. They are both disliked for al-Ẓuhr in a city on Friday.

He calls to prayer and performs the iqāmah for a missed prayer, likewise for the first of a number of missed prayers and it is disliked to leave the iqāmah not the adhan for the rest if the place of making them up is unified.

If one hears the proper sunnah of it then he refrains and repeats similar to it. He says "*lā ḥawla wa lā quwwata illa billāh*[205]" in the two callings[206] and "*ṣadaqta wa bararta*[207]" or "*mā shā Allah*[208]" at the saying of the caller to prayer "*aṣ-ṣalātu khayrun min an-nawm*" then he supplicates with "*al-wasīlah*[209]" so he says "Oh Allah, Lord of this complete call and established prayer, grant Muhammad al-wasīlah and virtue and send him to the praiseworthy station that You have promised him."

---

204 The adhan [Maraqi al-Falah, page 119].

205 There is no power or might except with Allah.

206 *Ḥayya ʿala al-ṣalāh* and *Ḥayya ʿala al-falāḥ* (Come to the prayer and come to success).

207 You have spoken the truth and been honest.

208 What Allah wills.

209 The highest place in Heaven for the Prophet Muhammad ﷺ [Al-Tirmidhi, 3612; Abu Dawud, 523; Al-Nasa'i, 678].

........................................................................................................

........................................................................................................

........................................................................................................

........................................................................................................

........................................................................................................

........................................................................................................

........................................................................................................

........................................................................................................

### Section of the Conditions of the Prayer and its Pillars

There must be twenty-seven things for the validity of the prayer:

1. Purity from legal impurity.
2. Purity of the body,
3. clothing,
4. and place from any impurity that is not excused even in the area of the feet, hands, knees, and forehead according to the soundest opinion.
5. Covering nakedness. Seeing it from his collar or the bottom of his hem does not harm.
6. Facing the qiblah. Therefore, for the one in Mecca who is looking[210] his obligation is facing it[211] exactly, and for the one who is not looking, its direction even if he is in Mecca according to the sound opinion.
7. The time and,
8. belief of its entering.
9. Intention.
10. The *taḥrīmah*[212]

---

210 At the Kaaba.

211 lit. hitting it

212 An utterance using Allah's name to initiate the prayer.

.......................................................................................................

.......................................................................................................

.......................................................................................................

.......................................................................................................

.......................................................................................................

.......................................................................................................

.......................................................................................................

a. without a break

b. performing the taḥrīmah standing before his inclination for bowing

c. not delaying the intention after the taḥrīmah

d. pronouncing the taḥrīmah so that he can hear himself according to the soundest opinion.

11. The intention to follow for the follower.

12. Specifying of the farḍ.

13. Specifying of the wājib, specification is not conditional for the voluntary.

14. Standing for other than the voluntary.

15. Recitation, even one verse, in two units of the farḍ and every unit of the voluntary and *al-Witr*. There is nothing specified from the Quran for the validity of the prayer. The one praying behind the imam does not recite, rather he listens attentively and remains silent, if he recites it is prohibitively disliked.

16. Bowing.

17. Prostration on that which he feels the shape of and his forehead settles on, even on his hand or the edge of his garment as long as the area of its[213] placing is pure.

18. He must prostrate on the hard part of his nose[214] and his forehead, restricting it to the nose is not valid unless due to an excuse in his forehead.

---

213 His hand or corner of his garment [Maraqi al-Falah, page 131].

214 Because the tip of his nose is not an area of prostration [Maraqi al-Falah, page 131].

19. The area of prostration must not be elevated above the place of the feet by more than half an arm's length (*dhirāᶜ*)[215]. If it is more than half an arm's length the prostration does not suffice unless due to congestion where he prostrated in it on the back of a person praying his[216] prayer.

20. Placing the hands and knees according to the sound opinion, and something from the toes on the ground whilst in the state of prostrating. Placing the outer of the foot does not suffice.

21. The preceding of bowing before prostration.

22. Raising from prostration to close to sitting according to the soundest opinion.

23. Returning to prostration.

24. The final sitting for the length of the *tashahhud*[217].

25. Delaying it[218] until after the pillars.

26. Performance of them[219] awake.

27. Knowledge of the method of the prayer and what it contains of obligatory aspects in a manner where he can distinguish them from the sunnah aspects, and belief that it[220] is obligatory in order that he doesn't perform a voluntary prayer with an obligatory one.

---

215 An arm's length (*dhirāᶜ*) is approximately 46cm. It is measured from the top of the middle finger to the elbow.

216 The prostrater.

217 See: Section on the Method of the Prayer

218 The tashahhud.

219 The pillars.

220 That specific prayer.

..........

..........

..........

..........

..........

..........

..........

..........

The pillars are four from what was mentioned:

1. Standing.
2. Recitation.
3. Bowing.
4. Prostration.

It was said: The final sitting for the amount of the tashahhud. The remaining of them are conditions, some of them are classed as a condition for the validity of initiating the prayer and it is that which is external to it[221], and the rest are classed as a condition for the continuity of its validity.

---

221 The prayer.

........................................................................................................................

........................................................................................................................

........................................................................................................................

........................................................................................................................

........................................................................................................................

........................................................................................................................

........................................................................................................................

........................................................................................................................

## Section of Things Connected to the Conditions of the Prayer and its Branches

The prayer is permitted on a piece of felt, the upper side being pure and the lower side of it being impure, on a pure garment whose inner lining is impure as long as it is not interwoven, on a pure edge[222] even if the impure edge moves with his movement according to the sound opinion. If one of the ends of his turban becomes impure and he throws it down whilst keeping the pure one on his head and the impure one does not move with his movement; the prayer is permitted. If it moves, it is not permitted.

The one who does not find that which removes impurity prays with it[223] and no repetition is binding upon him. Nor upon the one who does not find that which covers his nakedness not even silk, tall grass, or mud. Thus, if he finds it even if with permission[224] and a quarter of it is pure, his prayer naked is not valid. He is given the option if less than a quarter is pure. His prayer in a totally impure garment is more preferable than his prayer naked. If he finds that which covers part of his nakedness using it is obligatory and he covers the front and back private parts, if he can only cover one of them it is has been said "he covers the back" and it has been said "the front." It is recommended that the prayer of a naked person is done sat down with indications stretching his feet towards the qiblah, but if he prays standing with indications or with bowing and prostration it is valid.

The nakedness of a man is what is between the navel and the end of the knee[225] and a slave girl exceeds him with the stomach and lower back. The entire body[226]

222 Of a spread, mat, or garment [Maraqi al-Falah, page 135].

223 The impurity.

224 If he does not have permission to use the garment, he prays naked.

225 Ibn Quṭlūbughā said, "The sounder opinion is that the knee is part of the thigh." [Al-Tashih wa al-Tarjih, page 158]. Thus, if a man prays with his knees uncovered, it will be valid according to the sounder opinion due to a quarter of the limb not being exposed..

226 A'ishah (may Allah be pleased with her) narrated that Asma bint Abu Bakr entered upon the Messenger of Allah ﷺ wearing a thin dress. The Messenger of Allah ﷺ turned away from her and said, "Oh Asma, when a woman reaches the age of puberty, nothing should be seen of her except this and this" – and he pointed to his face and hands. [Abu Dawud 4104, Al-Marasil Abu Dawud 437, Al-Tabarani in Al-Awsat 8394, Al-Bayhaqi 3343, Majma' al-Zawa'id 8782]. Declared good due to

of a free woman is nakedness except her face and hands[227] and her feet[228].

corroborating chains by Al-Bayhaqi, Al-Dhahabi, Ibn Hajar al-Asqalani, Al-Zayla'i, Nur al-Din al-Haythami, Husayn al-Darani, and Albani.

It was narrated with a sound chain of transmission that Ibn Umar (may Allah be pleased with both of them) said regarding the verse, '*They should not display their adornment except what appears (naturally)* (24:31)': "The apparent adornment is the eyeliner (i.e. the face) and the ring (i.e. the hands)." [Al-Musannaf li Ibn Abi Shaybah, Book of Marriage, 17290] A similar statement has been soundly reported from Ibn Abbas [Al-Musannaf li Ibn Abi Shaybah, Book of Marriage, 17297].

227 The following has also been mentioned by Hanafi jurists:
"There is no harm in him looking at her face and her hand but he does not look at other than them and this is the statement of Abu Hanifah. Allah said, '*Tell the believing women to lower their gazes, preserve their private parts, and not to display their adornment except what appears from it*' the Quranic exegetes have explained "what is appears from it" to mean kohl (eyeliner) and the ring. Kohl is the adornment of the face, and the ring is the adornment of the hand so a dispensation was made for these two adornments" [Al-Asl, Kitab al-Istihsan].

"Fear of temptation (*fitnah*) could be by looking at her clothing also... then there is no doubt that it is permitted to look at her clothing and fear of temptation is not considered in that, so likewise at her face and her hand. Al-Hasan bin Ziyad narrated from Abu Hanifah that it is permitted to look at her foot and this is what Al-Tahawi mentioned" [Al-Mabsut, Kitab al-Istihsan].

"It is rationally valid that looking at the face of a woman is lawful if it is without sexual desire but lowering the gaze and refraining from looking is more courteous and purer... and that which indicates that a woman does not cover her face and that a man should not intentionally look at the face of a woman except in a time of need is the statement of the Messenger of Allah ﷺ to Ali (may Allah be pleased with him), 'You only have the first (glance) and you do not have the other (glance)'... It is better for a young girl and superior for her to conceal her face and hands from men, not because it is prohibited and it is an act of disobedience to her, but from what is feared from it of causing sexual desire and the occurrence of seduction with her... Also, what indicates that the face and hands are rationally valid not to be nakedness is that a woman cannot pray with her nakedness exposed and it is permitted for her to pray with her face, hands, and feet exposed" [Ta'wilat Ahl al-Sunnah, Surah al-Nur, 31].

"'*...except what appears from it.*' Except what custom and human nature is based on exposing of it, i.e. the face, hands, and feet because there is clear undue hardship in covering them. That is because a woman finds no way out of moving things with her hands and the need to expose her face especially in court testimonies, court cases, and marriage, and she is forced to walk in the streets and to expose her feet especially the poor women" [Madarik al-Tanzil, Surah al-Nur, 31].

However, it is prohibited for a marriageable man to look at these areas if there is fear of sexual desire.

228 Due to the generality of the necessity [Maraqi al-Falah, page 137].

The uncovering of a quarter of a limb from the limbs of nakedness prevents the validity of the prayer. If the uncovering is divided amongst the limbs of nakedness and the sum of what is divided reaches a quarter of the smallest of the uncovered limbs it prevents[229], and if not, then no.

Whoever is unable to face the qiblah due to an illness, or he is unable to alight from his riding-beast, or fears an enemy, then his qiblah is the direction of his ability and safety. Whoever the qiblah becomes obscure for and has no-one to inform him and no mihrab[230] he investigates and no repetition is binding upon him if he makes an error. If he knows of his error in his prayer then he turns and builds[231]. If he begins without investigation and knows after his finishing[232] that he was right, then it is valid. But if he knows of his being right whilst in it, then it is ruined, just as if he never knew of his being right whatsoever. If a group of people investigated different directions and they are unaware of the state of their imam, then it suffices them.

229 The validity of the prayer [Maraqi al-Falah, page 137].
230 A niche in the mosque that indicates the qiblah.
231 On what he has already performed with his investigation [Maraqi al-Falah, page 139].
232 The prayer [Maraqi al-Falah, page 139].

..............................................................................................................

..............................................................................................................

..............................................................................................................

..............................................................................................................

..............................................................................................................

..............................................................................................................

..............................................................................................................

..............................................................................................................

## Section Regarding Clarification of the Wājib of Prayer

It is eighteen things:

1. Recitation of *al-Fātiḥah* and,
2. adding a chapter or three verses in two unspecified units of the farḍ[233], every unit of al-Witr, and the voluntary.
3. Specifying recitation[234] in the first two units.
4. To do *al-Fātiḥah* before the chapter.
5. Adding the nose to the forehead in prostration.
6. Performance of the second prostration in every unit before moving on to something else.
7. Calm composure in the pillars[235].
8. The first sitting.
9. Recitation of the *tashahhud*[236] in it[237] according to the sound opinion.

---

233 One of the five obligatory daily prayers.

234 Of *al-Fātiḥah* and the chapter.

235 By relaxing of the limbs in bowing and prostration until the joints are calm [Maraqi al-Falah, page 142].

236 See: Section on the Method of the Prayer

237 The first sitting.

........................................................................................................

........................................................................................................

........................................................................................................

........................................................................................................

........................................................................................................

........................................................................................................

........................................................................................................

........................................................................................................

10. Recitation of it[238] in the final sitting.

11. Getting up for the third[239] without any delay after the tashahhud.

12. The utterance of "*al-salām*[240]" without "ᶜ*alaykum.*"

13. The supplication (*qunūt*) of al-Witr.

14. The *takbīrs*[241] of the two Eid prayers.

15. Specifying the takbīr for the opening of every prayer, not just the two Eid prayers specifically.

16. The *takbīrah* of bowing in the second unit of the two Eid prayers.

17. The audibility of the imam with his recitation in al-Fajr, the first two units of the two ᶜishā's[242] even if being made up, the Friday prayer, the two Eid prayers, *tarāwīḥ*[243] prayers, and the witr prayer in Ramadan.

18. Making it silent[244] in al-Ẓuhr and al-ᶜAṣr, in what is after the first two units of the two ᶜishā's, and voluntary daytime prayers. The one praying alone is given the choice in what is audible just like the one performing voluntary prayers at night.

If a person omits the chapter in the first two units of al-ᶜIshā' then he reads it in the last two. If he leaves al-Fātiḥah he does not repeat it in the last two.

238 The tashahhud.
239 The third unit of the prayer.
240 Twice, one on the right and one on the left [Maraqi al-Falah, page 143].
241 Takbīr is to utter the statement "*Allāhu akbar*" or what is similar to it.
242 Al-Maghrib and al-ᶜIshā' [Maraqi al-Falah, page 144].
243 See: Section on Tarāwīḥ.
244 According to *Ẓāhir al-Riwāyah* it is only wājib for the imam, see: [Hashiyah al-Tahtawi, Section of Sunnahs of the Prayer].

..........

..........

..........

..........

..........

..........

## Section Clarifying the Sunnahs of the Prayer

They are fifty-one:

1. Raising the hands for the taḥrīmah adjacent to the ears for a man and a slave girl,
2. but adjacent to the shoulders for a free woman.
3. Spreading the fingers[245].
4. The coupling of the *iḥrām*[246] of the follower with the *iḥrām* of his imam.
5. A man's placing his right hand over the left underneath his navel. The description of the placing is that he puts the inner palm of the right over the outer of his left palm making a circle with his small finger and his thumb over the wrist.
6. A woman's placing of her hands on her chest without making a circle.
7. The *thanāʾ*[247].
8. The *taʿawwudh*[248] for the recitation.
9. Saying "*bismillāhir-raḥmānir-raḥīm*"[249], at the beginning of every unit.

---

245 Not completely apart, but not closed together [Maraqi al-Falah, page 146].

246 The opening takbīr, also called the *taḥrīmah* as previously mentioned.

247 Opening words of praise, see page 77.

248 Saying "I seek refuge with Allah from the accursed Satan."

249 Saying "In the name of Allah, most compassionate, most merciful."

..........................................................................................................

..........................................................................................................

..........................................................................................................

..........................................................................................................

..........................................................................................................

..........................................................................................................

10. Saying "*Āmīn*[250]."

11. The *taḥmīd*[251].

12. Saying them silently.

13. Keeping a straight back when doing the *taḥrīmah* without tilting the head.

14. The imam saying the *takbīr* and the *tasmīʿ*[252] aloud.

15. Spreading the feet in the standing position the amount of four fingers[253].

16. That the chapter that is joined with al-Fātiḥah is from lengthy separated chapters[254] in al-Fajr and al-Ẓuhr, from its medium in al-ʿAṣr and al-ʿIshāʾ, and from its short in al-Maghrib if he is resident. If he is a traveller then he reads any chapter that he wishes.

17. Lengthening the first unit in al-Fajr only.

18. The takbīr for bowing and

19. its *tasbīḥ*[255] three times.

20. Grabbing his knees with his hands.

21. Spreading his fingers, but a woman does not spread them.

---

250 Amen. A supplication meaning "so be it."
251 Saying "Our Lord, to you belongs all praise" or its equivalent.
252 Saying "Allah heard the one who praises him."
253 Due to it being closer to humility [Maraqi al-Falah, page 148].
254 The separated chapters are the last seventh of the Quran [Maraqi al-Falah, page 148].
255 Glorifying Allah with invocation, usually by saying "Glory be to Allah."

..........................................................................................

..........................................................................................

..........................................................................................

..........................................................................................

..........................................................................................

..........................................................................................

..........................................................................................

..........................................................................................

22. Erecting his legs[256].

23. Spreading his back.

24. Levelling his head with his backside.

25. Raising from bowing[257] and

26. standing after it with calm composure.

27. Placing his knees, then his hands, then his face for prostration and

28. the opposite of it for rising.

29. The takbīr of prostration.

30. The takbīr of rising from it.

31. The prostration being between his hands.

32. The tasbīḥ for it three times.

33. A man's distancing his stomach away from his knees, his elbows away from his sides, and his arms away from the ground.

34. A woman's lowering and attaching of her stomach with her thighs.

35. *Al-qawmah*[258].

256 This needs more investigation due it not being mentioned in the primary texts or *Ẓāhir al-Riwāyah.*

257 Al-Kamal and others chose the opinion that raising from bowing and prostration is wājib just like calm composure in both of them. Ibn Abidin said "It is in accordance with the legal evidences even if the famously known opinion in the school is the narration of it being sunnah" [Radd al-Muhtar, Section of Sunnahs of the Prayer (320/1)].

258 The completing of the rising in between the two prostrations, rising from prostration to close to sitting is *farḍ*, so the completion of it is *sunnah* [Maraqi al-Falah, page 151].

........................................................................................................

........................................................................................................

........................................................................................................

........................................................................................................

........................................................................................................

........................................................................................................

........................................................................................................

........................................................................................................

36. The sitting between the two prostrations.

37. Placing the hands on the thighs for what is between the two prostrations like the state of the tashahhud.

38. Spreading his left leg and erecting the right[259].

39. The sitting of a woman on her buttocks.

40. Pointing with the index finger during the testimony according to the sound opinion. He raises it during the negation and lowers it during the affirmation.

41. Recitation of al-Fātiḥah in what is after the first two units.

42. Sending blessings *(al-ṣalāh)* upon the Prophet ﷺ in the final sitting.

43. Supplication with what resembles the wordings of the Quran and Sunnah[260] not the speech of people.

44. Turning to the right, then to the left with the two salutations[261].

45. The intention of the imam with the two salutations is the men[262], guardian angels, the righteous jinn according to the sounder position[263].

---

259 And pointing his toes towards the qiblah as has been transmitted from Ibn Umar (may Allah be pleased with both of them) [Maraqi al-Falah, page 152].

260 The prophetic traditions i.e. the Hadith

261 Because the Prophet ﷺ would give salutations on his right then say "Al-salamu alaykum wa rahmatullah" until the whiteness of his right cheek was visible, and on his left then say "Al-salamu alaykum wa rahmatullah" until the whiteness of his left cheek was visible [Maraqi al-Falah, page 154], [Al-Nasa'i, 1325].

262 And women and children [Maraqi al-Falah, page 154].

263 It was said that he only intends them with the first salutation, and it was said that indicating towards them is sufficient [Maraqi al-Falah, page 155].

.......................................................................................................

.......................................................................................................

.......................................................................................................

.......................................................................................................

.......................................................................................................

.......................................................................................................

.......................................................................................................

46. The intention of the follower is his imam in his direction, if he is parallel to him then he intends him for both salutations, including the people, guardian angels, and righteous jinn.

47. The intention of a person praying alone is only the angels.

48. Making the second salutation quieter than the first[264].

49. Its[265] coupling with the salutation of the imam.

50. Starting with the right[266].

51. The latecomer's waiting for the finishing of the imam.

---

264 The reason why needs investigation. It has only been mentioned in a one or two other texts, perhaps it was a form of distinguishing between the two salutations so that the follower and latecomer know the position of the imam.

265 The salutation of the follower [Maraqi al-Falah, page 155].

266 This has already been mentioned previously.

## Section on the Etiquettes of the Prayer

From its etiquettes are:

1. The removing of a man[267] his hands from his sleeves at the time of the takbīr.
2. The person praying looking at the place of his prostration when standing, the outer of the foot when bowing, the tip of his nose when prostrating, his bosom when sitting, and the shoulders when giving salutations.
3. Suppressing coughing as much as possible.
4. Concealing his mouth when yawning.
5. Standing when "*ḥayya ʿala al-falāḥ*" is said.
6. The starting of the imam when "*qad qāmatiṣ-ṣalāh*" is said.

---

267 A woman covers her hands to avoid the exposure of her arms [Maraqi al-Falah, page 156].

........................................................................................................

........................................................................................................

........................................................................................................

........................................................................................................

........................................................................................................

........................................................................................................

........................................................................................................

........................................................................................................

## Section on the Method of the Prayer

If a man wants to enter the prayer, he removes his hands from his sleeves[268] then raises them adjacent to his ears, then says "*Allāhu akbar*" without elongation[269] making intention. Initiation is valid with any *dhikr*[270] that is purely for Allah (exalted is He) like "*subḥānallāh*" and in Persian if he is incapable of Arabic, if he is capable then his initiation is not valid in Persian[271], nor his recitation in Persian according to the sounder opinion. Then he places his right over his left underneath his navel just after the *taḥrīmah* without any delay commencing which is that he says "*subḥānak allāhumma wa biḥamdika wa tabārakasmuka wa taʿālā jadduka wa lā ilāha ghayruk*[272]" every person who prays does this commencing[273]. Then he seeks refuge[274] silently for the recitation, thus the latecomer performs it not the follower but it is delayed until

268 As opposed to a woman or a state of necessity [Maraqi al-Falah, page 157].

269 If he elongates its hamzah he hasn't initiated the prayer and it will be invalid because of it during the prayer [Maraqi al-Falah, page 157].

270 Utterance of remembrance.

271 The sound opinion is that initiation is valid in any language other than Arabic even if he is capable (as opposed to recitation of the Quran) but it is prohibitively disliked to do so. See: [Radd al-Muhtar, Chapter of the Prayer, Additional Matters When He Recites in Persian or Rescites the Torah or Gospel] and [Hashiyah al-Tahtawi, Section on the method of the prayer].

272 Glory be to You, Allah, and with Your praise, blessed is Your name, exalted is Your majesty and there is no god other than You.

273 Whether praying behind the imam or not as long as the imam hasn't started to recite the Quran [Maraqi al-Falah, page 158].

274 With Allah from the accursed Satan [Maraqi al-Falah, page 158].

after the takbīrs of the two Eid prayers. Then he says "*bismillāhir-raḥmānir-raḥīm*" silently and he says this in every unit before al-Fātiḥah only. Then he recites al-Fātiḥah and the imam and the follower say "āmīn" silently. Then he recites a chapter or three verses. Then he says "*Allāhu akbar*" bowing[275] with calm composure levelling his head with his behind, grabbing his knees with his hands, spreading his fingers[276]. He makes tasbīḥ in it three times and that is the lowest of it[277]. Then he raises his head and maintains calm composure saying "*samiᶜallāhu liman ḥamidah*[278]" "*rabbanā lakal-ḥamd*[279]" if he is the imam or praying alone, the follower suffices with the taḥmīd. Then he says "*Allāhu akbar*" whilst falling to the ground for prostration. Then he places his knees, then his hands, then his face between his palms and prostrates with his nose and his forehead with calm composure glorifying Allah three times, and that is the lowest of it. He distances his stomach from his thighs and his upper arms from his armpits when there is no congestion, pointing his fingers and toes towards the qiblah. A woman lowers and joins her stomach to her thighs. Every person who prays sits between the two prostrations placing his hands on his thighs with calm composure then he says "*Allāhu akbar*," prostrates with calm composure, glorifies Allah in it three times, distances his stomach from his thighs and reveals his upper arms. Then he raises his head whilst saying "*Allāhu akbar*" for rising without resting on the ground with his hands and without sitting. The second unit is like the first except that he does not do the thanā' or taᶜawwudh. The raising of hands is not sunnah apart from at the opening of every prayer, for the takbīr of the qunūt in al-Witr, the additional takbīrs in the two Eid prayers, when he sees the Kaaba, when he greets the Black Stone, when he stands on al-Safa and

275 Thus, he starts with takbīr with the starting of bending and he ends it with its ending [Maraqi al-Falah, page 159].

276 A woman does not spread her fingers [Maraqi al-Falah, page 159].

277 The lowest perfection of the sunnah plural [Maraqi al-Falah, page 159].

278 "Allah heard the one who praises him."

279 "Our Lord, praise belongs to you."

al-Marwah, when stopping at Arafah and Muzdalifah, after stoning the first pillar and the middle one[280], and when making tasbīh after the prayers. When a man finishes the two prostrations of the second unit he spreads his left leg, sits on it, erects his right leg, directs its toes towards the qiblah, places his hands upon his thighs, spreads his fingers (a woman sits on her buttocks), and recites the tashahhud of Ibn Masᶜūd (may Allah be pleased with him). He points with his index finger in the testimony; he raises it for the negation and lowers it for the affirmation. He does not do more than the tashahhud in the first sitting, which is:

*At-taḥiyyātu lillāhi waṣ-ṣalawātu waṭ-ṭayyibāt, as-salāmu ᶜalayka ayyuhan-nabii wa raḥmatullahi wa barakātuhu, as-salāmu ᶜalaynā wa ᶜalā ᶜibādillāhiṣ-ṣāliḥīn, ash-hadu allā ilāha ill-allāh wa ash-hadu anna muḥammadan ᶜabduhu wa rasūluhu.*[281]

He recites al-Fātiḥah in what is after the first two units, then he sits and recites the tashahhud, then he sends blessings on the Prophet ﷺ, then he supplicates with what resembles the Quran and Sunnah, then he gives salutations on his right and left thus he says:

"*As-salāmu ᶜalaykum wa raḥmatullāh*" intending whoever is with him as preceded[282].

---

280 At Mina.

281 Salutations belong to Allah, prayers and excellent words. Peace be on you oh Prophet, and the mercy of Allah and His blessings. Peace be upon us and upon Allah's righteous slaves. I testify that there is no god except Allah and that Muhammad is His slave and messenger.

282 In the previous section.

............................................................

............................................................

............................................................

............................................................

............................................................

............................................................

............................................................

## Section of the Imamate

It is better than the adhan. Praying in congregation is sunnah for free men when there is no excuse. The conditions for the validity of the imamah for healthy men are six things:

1. Islam.
2. Puberty.
3. Intellect.
4. Masculinity.
5. Recitation[283].
6. Safety from excuses such as nose-bleeding[284], stammering with the letter *fā'* or *tā'*, and a lisp. Also, safety from the absence of a condition such as purification and covering nakedness.

The conditions for the validity of following are fourteen things:

1. The intention of the follower of following coupled with his[285] taḥrīmah.
2. A man's intention for the imamate is a condition for the validity of women following him.

283 With the memorisation of one verse.
284 Chronic nose-bleeding [Maraqi al-Falah, page 166].
285 The follower's, either literally or legally.

3. The preceding of the imam with his heel in front of the follower.
4. That he is not at a lower state than the follower is[286].
5. That the imam is not praying a farḍ other than his farḍ.
6. That he is not a resident for the traveller after the prayer time in a four-unit prayer[287],
7. and not a latecomer.
8. That a row of women does not separate between the imam and the follower.
9. That a river that boats pass through does not separate,
10. nor a road that a carriage passes through,
11. nor a wall that the knowledge of the movements of the imam would become obscure, if it is not obscure due to hearing or seeing then the following is valid according to the sound opinion.
12. That the imam is not riding and the follower on foot or riding an animal other than the animal of his imam.
13. That he is not in a boat and the imam in another not connected to it.
14. That the follower does not know from the state of his imam an

---

286 e.g. He is doing a voluntary prayer and the follower is doing an obligatory prayer [Maraqi al-Falah, page 167]. Likewise, if the imam is praying with indications and the follower is bowing and prostrating, though Imam Zufar permits this.

287 Thus, if they were both to miss a four-unit prayer and decide to make it up together, only the traveller could be the imam due to his first sitting being farḍ and the resident's being wājib.

........................................................................................................................

........................................................................................................................

........................................................................................................................

........................................................................................................................

........................................................................................................................

........................................................................................................................

........................................................................................................................

........................................................................................................................

invalidator in the opinion of the follower, such as the exiting of blood or vomit and he[288] did not repeat his wudu.

The following of a person who made wudu of a person who made tayammum, a person who washed of a person who wiped, a person standing with a person sitting and a hunchback, a person praying with indications of someone similar, and a person praying a voluntary prayer with a person praying an obligatory prayer is valid.

If the invalidity of his imam's prayer becomes apparent then he repeats it. The imam must inform people about the repeating of their prayer as much as possible according to the chosen opinion.

---

288 The imam.

........................................................................................................

........................................................................................................

........................................................................................................

........................................................................................................

........................................................................................................

........................................................................................................

........................................................................................................

........................................................................................................

## Section on Omission of Attending the Congregation

Attending the congregation is omitted due to one of eighteen things[289]:

1. Rain and,
2. Snow.[290]
3. Fear.
4. Darkness[291].

---

289 This is an exhaustive list, Ibn Abidin mentions in a poem: "The totality of excuses which has passed in the text and commentary are twenty which I versified in my saying: 'The excuses of missing the congregational prayer are twenty Which indeed I have inserted in the arrangement of verses like pearls, Sickness, infirmity, blindness, being crippled Rain, muddy ground then coldness that causes harm,

Amputation of a leg with a hand or within them
Paralysis, an old man's weakness and the intention to travel,
Fear of wealth, likewise of an oppressor
Or creditor, and desire to eat food that is present,
Wind at night, darkness, nursing a person with
Sickness, the compulsion of urine or faeces,
Then, occupation with nothing besides knowledge in
Some situations is an excuse that is considered.'"

[Radd al-Muhtar, Section of Congregational Prayer (1:581)].

290 Heavy rain and snow [Maraqi al-Falah, page 171].

291 Intense darkness according to the sound opinion [Maraqi al-Falah, page 171].

........................................................................................................

........................................................................................................

........................................................................................................

........................................................................................................

........................................................................................................

........................................................................................................

........................................................................................................

........................................................................................................

5. Imprisonment.
6. Blindness.
7. Paralysis.
8. Amputation of a hand and leg.
9. Illness.
10. Disability.
11. Mud.
12. Chronic illness.
13. Decrepitude.
14. Revising jurisprudence (*fiqh*)[292] with a group that he would miss[293].
15. The presence of food that his lower self desires[294].
16. Intending to travel.
17. Looking after a sick person.
18. Intensity of winds at night, not day.

If he fails to appear at the congregational prayer due to an excuse from its excuses that permit remaining behind, then he attains its reward.

---

292 Not grammar or language [Maraqi al-Falah, page 171].

293 Meaning that those he is revising with would go. It is better that this restriction is not added because he can still pray in congregation with the group that is with him. See: [Hashiyah al-Tahtawi, Section on Congregational Prayer].

294 Due to it occupying his mind [Maraqi al-Falah, page 171]. Likewise, other things that will occupy his mind can be added to this, such as a need to relieve himself.

........................................................................................................

........................................................................................................

........................................................................................................

........................................................................................................

........................................................................................................

........................................................................................................

........................................................................................................

........................................................................................................

## Section on Clarification of who has More Right to the Imamate and the Order of the Rows

If the house owner, person of position[295], or person of authority is not among those who are present then the most knowledgeable has the most right to the imamate, then the most proficient in recital, then the most godfearingly cautious, then the oldest, then the best in character, then the one with the most handsome face, then the one with the most honourable lineage, then the one with the best voice. If they are all equal then lots are drawn or the choice goes to the people, if they differ then consideration is with what the majority choose. If they put forward someone who is not the most befitting then they have committed a wrong.

The imamate of a slave, a blind person, a Bedouin, a bastard, an ignorant person, a sinner, an innovator, lengthening the prayer, a congregation of naked people, and of women[296] is disliked. If women do perform a congregation then the female imam stands in the middle of them like naked people[297].

One person stands to the right of the imam and any more stand behind him. The men line up in a row, then children, then hermaphrodites, then women[298].

---

295 i.e. The boss or local imam.

296 Solely.

297 Like a naked imam for a naked congregation.

298 Due to the hadith: "The best of rows for men are the first ones, the worst are the last ones, and the best of rows for women are the last ones, the worst are the first ones." [Abu Dawud, 678 (Sahih)]

.........................................................................................................

.........................................................................................................

.........................................................................................................

.........................................................................................................

.........................................................................................................

.........................................................................................................

.........................................................................................................

.........................................................................................................

## Section on What the Follower Does After his Imam's Finishing of a Wājib and Other Than it[299]

If the imam gave salutations before the finishing of the follower of the tashahhud, he completes it. If the imam raised his head before the tasbīḥ of the follower three times in bowing or prostration, he follows him. If the imam added a prostration or stood before the final sitting forgetfully, then the follower does not follow him and if he[300] restricts it[301], he[302] gives salutations alone[303]. If the imam stood up before the final sitting forgetfully, then the follower waits, but if the follower gave salutations before his imam restricted the extra unit with a prostration, then his farḍ is ruined[304]. The salutation (*salām*) of the follower after the tashahhud of the imam before his[305] salutation is disliked.

---

299 Meaning, what he does not do after the imam has completed the wājib.

300 The imam [Maraqi al-Falah, page 179].

301 The extra unit with a prostration [Maraqi al-Falah, page 179].

302 The follower [Maraqi al-Falah, page 179].

303 To leave the prayer in a proper manner even though his prayer is ruined. However, the follower should not wait for the imam to finish because the imam has gone on to something other than the prayer.

304 The prayer of the follower is ruined because he has isolated himself with the obligatory pillar of sitting in the state of following the imam, just like it will be ruined if the imam restricts the extra unit with a prostration due to leaving the final sitting [Maraqi al-Falah, page 179].

305 The imam's.

## Section on the Description of Transmitted Remembrances Done After the Farḍ Prayer

Getting up to perform the sunnah connected to the farḍ is sunnah[306]. It was narrated from Shams al-A'immah al-Hulwani: "There is no harm in recitation of litanies between the farḍ and the sunnah." After his salutation, it is recommended for the imam to move to the direction of his left to perform voluntary prayers after the farḍ, and that he faces the people after it[307]. They say "*astaghfirullāh*" three times, recite *ayah al-kursi*[308], *al-Muᶜawwadhāt*[309], say "*subḥānallāh*" thirty-three times, likewise "*alḥamdulillāh*" and "*Allāhu akbar*", then they say "*lā ilāha ill-allāhu waḥdahu lā sharīka lah, lahul-mulk, wa lahul-ḥamd, wa huwa ᶜalā kulli shay'in qadīr*[310]", then they supplicate for themselves and the Muslims raising their hands, then they wipe their faces with them at the end of it.

---

306 This is if he prayṣ his sunnah in the mosque for example, as for if he wants to go home to perform them, then the interruption is not disliked [Hashiyah al-Tahtawi, Section of Remembrances After the Prayer].
307 The voluntary prayer [Maraqi al-Falah, page 181].
308 Verse 255 of Surah al-Baqarah.
309 The last two verses of the Quran.
310 There is no god other than Allah solely, He has no partner, the kingdom belongs to Him, praise belongs to Him, and He is powerful over all things.

## Section of what Ruins the Prayer

It is sixty-eight things:

1. A word, even forgetfully[311] or
2. mistakenly[312].
3. Supplication that resembles our speech.
4. The salām with the intention of greeting, even forgetfully.
5. Returning the salām with his tongue or
6. by shaking hands.
7. Excessive action.
8. Moving the chest away from the qiblah.
9. Eating something from outside of his mouth, even if small.
10. Eating what is between his teeth and it is the amount of a chickpea.
11. His drinking.
12. Coughing without an excuse.
13. Grumbling.
14. Moaning.

311 Thinking that he is not in prayer [Maraqi al-Falah, page 183].
312 Even if it is not beneficial like "Oh" [Maraqi al-Falah, page 183].

..........................................................................................

..........................................................................................

..........................................................................................

..........................................................................................

..........................................................................................

..........................................................................................

..........................................................................................

..........................................................................................

15. Sighing.
16. His crying becoming loud due to pain or,
17. a calamity, not from the remembrance of Heaven or Hell.
18. Responding to a person who sneezes with "*yarḥamukallāh.*[313]"
19. The reply to one who asks about a partner[314] with "*lā ilāha ill-allāh,*"
20. to bad news with saying "*innā lillāhi wa innā ilayhi rājiʿūn*[315]*,*"
21. good news with "alḥamdulillāh,"
22. and wonderous news with "*lā ilāha ill-allāh*" or,
23. "subḥānallāh."
24. Every thing that a reply is intended with such as "*Oh John, take the book.*" (19:12)
25. A person in tayammum seeing water.
26. The completion of the time period for a person wiping over leather socks and
27. removing it.
28. The illiterate person learning one verse[316].
29. The naked person finding a cover.

---

313 May Allah have mercy upon you.
314 For Allah.
315 Indeed we belong to Allah and we are surely returning to Him.
316 Meaning, someone who has not memorised any of the Quran then hears or sees a verse in the prayer.

........................................................................................................................

........................................................................................................................

........................................................................................................................

........................................................................................................................

........................................................................................................................

........................................................................................................................

........................................................................................................................

........................................................................................................................

30. The ability of bowing and prostrating for someone praying with indications.
31. Remembering a missed prayer for the person of order[317].
32. Delegating someone who is not eligible to be an imam.
33. The rising of the sun in al-Fajr,
34. its moving from the zenith in the two Eid prayers and,
35. the entrance of the time of al-ᶜAṣr in the Friday prayer.
36. A splint falling off a healed limb.
37. The disappearance of the excuse of the excused person.
38. Breaking wudu intentionally or
39. due to someone else's doing[318].
40. Unconsciousness.
41. Insanity.
42. Major legal impurity due to looking or
43. a wet-dream.
44. A sexually desirable woman becoming parallel in a total prayer sharing a taḥrīmah in a unified place without a barrier and he intended leading her[319].

---

317 See: Section of Making up Missed Prayers, page 125.

318 As opposed to minor legal impurity overtaking him because he can build with it [Maraqi al-Falah, page 187].

319 Thus, the prayer of the man will be invalid, not the woman's prayer. However, if she is under the age of sexual desirability and puberty, or is not parallel with him, or not in a full prayer e.g. the funeral prayer, or she is praying a different prayer, or

45. The appearance of nakedness from the one who is overcome by minor legal impurity, even if they are forced to do it such as a woman uncovering her arms for wudu.

46. His reciting of the Quran when going to or coming from performing wudu.

47. His remaining, in a waken state, the length of performing a pillar after being overcome by minor legal impurity.

48. His going past water close by for other water.

49. His leaving the mosque thinking he has broken wudu and

50. his going past the rows in other places with him thinking that.

51. His departure thinking that he is not in a state of wudu,

52. the time period of wiping has elapsed,

53. that he has a missed prayer to do, or

54. impurity on him, even if he does not leave the mosque. Starting the prayer again is better[320].

55. His interjecting to someone other than his imam.

56. Takbīr with the intention of moving to another prayer other than his prayer.

---

they are in different places, or there is a barrier between them, or the imam did not include her in his intention, or he gestured her to move back and she did not, then his prayer is valid.

320 Than building on a prayer that he has been overcome by ritual purity in. Points 45-54 are all related to building on the prayer when a person has unintentionally lost their wudu.

.........................................................................................

.........................................................................................

.........................................................................................

.........................................................................................

.........................................................................................

.........................................................................................

.........................................................................................

If any of the aforementioned occurs before the final sitting for the length of the tashahhud.

57. The following will also ruin it: Elongation of the *hamzah* in the takbīr.
58. Recitation from a copy of the Quran of what he has not memorised[321].
59. Performance of a pillar or the ability to perform it with exposure of nakedness or
60. preventative impurity.
61. The follower going ahead by a pillar that his imam did not take part in.
62. Following the imam in a prostration of forgetfulness for the latecomer.
63. Lack of repetition of the final sitting after performance of a core prostration[322] that he remembered after the sitting.
64. Lack of repetition of a pillar that he performed whilst sleeping.
65. The laughing out loud of the imam of a latecomer and
66. his[323] breaking wudu intentionally after the final sitting[324].

321 With Abu Hanifah. Abu Yusuf and Imam Muhammad said it is valid but with dislike due to simulation of the *People of the Book*. See: [Al-Bahr al-Ra'iq, Section on Disliked Actions in the Prayer].

322 Or a prostration of recitation [Maraqi al-Falah, page 192].

323 The imam.

324 The prayer of the latecomer would be invalid in these two scenarios, but not the prayer of the imam.

67. Saying the salām at the end of two units in other than a two-unit prayer thinking that he is a traveller, that it is the Friday prayer, that it is the *tarāwīḥ* prayer and it is actually al-ʿIshā', or

68. he has recently converted to Islam and thought that the farḍ was two units.

........................................................................................................

........................................................................................................

........................................................................................................

........................................................................................................

........................................................................................................

........................................................................................................

........................................................................................................

........................................................................................................

## Section on What Does Not Ruin the Prayer

If the person praying looks at something written and understands it, he eats what is between his teeth without excessive action and it is less than a chickpea, or a passer-by passes the place of his prostration, then the prayer is not ruined, even though the passer-by is sinful. It is not invalidated with his looking at the vagina of a divorced woman with sexual desire, even though revocation[325] is established.

325 The taking back of one's wife after a revocable divorce. This can be done by a verbal statement or sexual contact, one of the methods is that he looks at her inner vagina with sexual desire.

........................................................................................................

........................................................................................................

........................................................................................................

........................................................................................................

........................................................................................................

........................................................................................................

........................................................................................................

........................................................................................................

## Section on the Disliked Actions of the Prayer

Seventy-seven things are disliked for the person praying:

1. Leaving a wājib or
2. a sunnah intentionally such as
3. playing with his clothes or
4. his body,
5. flipping stones except once for prostration,
6. cracking fingers,
7. intertwining them,
8. placing one's hands on the hips,
9. and turning with his neck.
10. Sitting on his buttocks with his knees erected.
11. Spreading his arms on the floor.
12. Rolling his sleeves up his arms.[326]
13. His prayer in trousers[327] with his ability to wear a shirt.

326 If done out of arrogance or inside the prayer. This should not be confused with wearing short-sleeves, which is permitted without dislike.

327 Or in a sarong [Maraqi al-Falah, page 196]. Meaning without an upper garment.

14. Returning salutations with an indication.
15. Sitting cross-legged without an excuse.
16. Tying his hair up.
17. *Al-Iᶜtijār,* which is tying the head with a head-kerchief[328] and leaving the centre uncovered.
18. Drawing his garment together[329] and
19. its hanging down[330].
20. Wrapping up in it to the point where he cannot remove his arms.
21. Placing his garment under his right armpit and tossing its two ends on his left shoulder.
22. Recitation in other than the standing position.
23. Lengthening the first unit in voluntary prayer and
24. lengthening the second unit more than the first in all prayers.
25. Repetition of a chapter in one unit of the farḍ prayer.
26. Recitation of a chapter above the one that he read.
27. His separating of a chapter between two chapters that he read in two units.
28. Smelling fragrance and

---

328 Or wrapping a turban around his head [Maraqi al-Falah, page 197].

329 Meaning, his lifting it in front of him or behind him when he wants to prostrate [Maraqi al-Falah, page 197].

330 Out of arrogance and carelessness, it is not disliked with an excuse [Maraqi al-Falah, page 197].

.......................................................................................................

.......................................................................................................

.......................................................................................................

.......................................................................................................

.......................................................................................................

.......................................................................................................

.......................................................................................................

.......................................................................................................

29. wafting it with his garment or
30. a fan once or twice.
31. Diverting his fingers or
32. toes away from the qiblah in prostration and
33. in other than prostration.
34. Omission of placing the hands on the knees in bowing.
35. Yawning.
36. Closing his eyes[331] and
37. raising them to the sky.
38. Stretching.
39. A small amount of action.
40. Taking hold of a louse and
41. killing it.
42. Covering his nose and
43. his mouth.
44. Putting something in his mouth that prevents the sunnah recitation.
45. Prostration on the roll of his turban and
46. on a picture[332]and

331 Unless it aids concentration

332 That possess a soul [Maraqi al-Falah, page 201].

..........................................................................................

..........................................................................................

..........................................................................................

..........................................................................................

..........................................................................................

..........................................................................................

..........................................................................................

..........................................................................................

47. restricting it to the forehead without an excuse with the nose.
48. Prayer in the street,
49. public baths,
50. toilet,
51. graveyard,
52. someone else's land without their consent, and
53. close to an impurity.
54. Withholding one of the two filths[333] or
55. wind.
56. Prayer in worn-out clothes,
57. with the head uncovered unless done for humility and humbleness,
58. in the presence of food that he is inclined towards,
59. anything that busies the mind, and
60. interrupts humbleness.
61. Counting verses and
62. *tasbīḥ*[334] by hand.
63. The imam's standing in the mihrab,
64. above a place, or
65. the ground on his own.

---

333 Urine or faeces.
334 Glorifications such as saying 'subḥānallāh.'

........................................................................................................

........................................................................................................

........................................................................................................

........................................................................................................

........................................................................................................

........................................................................................................

........................................................................................................

66. Standing behind a row that has a gap.
67. Wearing a garment that has images on it.
68. That a picture is above his head,
69. behind him,
70. in front of him,
71. or at his side unless it is small, has the head cut off, or does not possess a soul.
72. That a clay oven is in front of him or,
73. a stove that has hot embers in it, or
74. people sleeping.
75. Wiping dirt from his forehead that does not harm him throughout the prayer.
76. Specifying a chapter with him not reciting any other unless to make it easy for him or to seek blessing from the recitation of the Prophet ﷺ.
77. Omission of using a barrier in a place that it is believed passing in front of the person praying will occur.

........................................................................................................

........................................................................................................

........................................................................................................

........................................................................................................

........................................................................................................

........................................................................................................

........................................................................................................

## Section on Using a Barrier and Repelling the Passer in Front of the Person Praying

If he thinks that his passing will occur, then it is recommended for him to plant a barrier that is the length of an arm's length or more with the thickness of a finger. The sunnah is that he comes close to it and places it on the side of one of his eyebrows, he does not face it directly. If he cannot find something that he can erect, then let him draw a line vertically[335] and they[336] said, "horizontally like a crescent."

Refraining from repelling the one who crosses is recommended. Repelling him with a signal or with tasbīḥ but it is disliked to join between them. He can repel him by raising his voice with recitation and she can repel him with a signal or by clapping with the outer fingers of the right hand on the surface of the palm of the left hand but she does not raise her voice because it is a temptation[337]. He does not fight the person crossing and what has been mentioned is interpreted to mean that it used to be when action was permitted[338] but it has definitely been abrogated.

---

335 A large number of early scholars prohibited the use of a line but the later scholars permitted it [Maraqi al-Falah, page 208].
336 The later scholars.
337 Not in and of itself, but if she stretches her voice with recitation or singing there is the possibility of temptation.
338 In the prayer, in the beginning of Islam.

### Section on What is not Disliked for the Person Praying

The following are not disliked:

1. Tying up the midsection.
2. Wearing a sword and what is similar as long as he does not become preoccupied with its movement[339].
3. Not placing his arms in a *farjiyyah*[340] or a *shuqqah*[341] according to the chosen opinion[342].
4. Facing a copy of the Quran, a sword hung up, the back of someone talking, a candle, or a lamp according to the sound opinion.
5. Prostration on a mat with pictures on which he does not prostrate.
6. Killing a snake or a scorpion that he fears their harm, even with numerous strikes and turning away from the qiblah according to the stronger view.

---

339 If it occupies him then it is disliked but not in a state of fighting [Maraqi al-Falah, page 211].

340 A loose garment usually made from broadcloth with two long wide sleeves.

341 Originally half of a garment, but means an oblong piece of cloth. See [Lanes Lexicon, *shiqqa*].

342 The correct opinion is that it is disliked due to it being like a hanging garment, this the stance held by Qadikhan and Al-Tahtawi. See: [Hashiyah al-Tahtawi, Section on Disliked Actions of the Prayer, page 474]. The main principle here is whether it disturbs the person praying or not.

........................................................................................................

........................................................................................................

........................................................................................................

........................................................................................................

........................................................................................................

........................................................................................................

........................................................................................................

........................................................................................................

There is no harm in:

7. Shaking his garment in order that it does not cling to his body in the bowing position.

8. Wiping dust or grass from his forehead after finishing the prayer or before finishing if it harms him or distracts him from the prayer.

9. Looking with the inner corner of his eyes without turning the face.

10. Praying on carpets, mats, and thick rugs. However, the prayer is better on the earth or what it[343] grows.

11. Repetition of a chapter in two units of voluntary prayer.

343 The earth.

........................................................................................................................

........................................................................................................................

........................................................................................................................

........................................................................................................................

........................................................................................................................

........................................................................................................................

........................................................................................................................

........................................................................................................................

## Section on What Necessitates Breaking the Prayer, What Allows it, and Other Than it From Delaying the Prayer and Leaving it

The prayer must be broken with the calling for help of a person in distress out to the person praying but not with the calling of one of his parents[344].

It is permitted to break it due to the theft of what is equivalent to one *dirham*[345] even if it belongs to someone else, fear of his sheep due to a wolf, or fear of the falling of a blind person into well or something similar.

If the midwife fears the death of the baby[346] she must delay the prayer, if not then there is no harm in her delaying the prayer and attending to the child. Likewise, if the traveller fears robbers or highwaymen it is permitted for him to delay the prayer of the time.

The one who abandons the prayer intentionally out of laziness is beaten severely until blood flows from him and is imprisoned until he prays it[347]. Likewise, the one who abandons fasting Ramadan but he is not killed unless he rejects or belittles either of them.

---

344 That are not calling for help because breaking the prayer is only permitted for a necessity [Maraqi al-Falah, page 214].

345 A silver coin weighing 2.975g.

346 Or loss of a limb or the mother [Maraqi al-Falah, page 215].

347 The correct opinion is that he is not beaten. See: [Radd al-Muhtar, Introduction of the Chapter of Prayer and Hashiyah al-Tahtawi, Section on What Necessitates Breaking the Prayer]. Likewise, the ruling is only to be applied by the authorities of legitimate Islamic governance for legitimate benefits.

## Section of al-Witr and its Rulings

The witr prayer is wājib[348]. It is three units with one set of salutations. He recites al-Fātiḥah and a chapter in every unit. He sits at the end of the first two of it, limits himself to the tashahhud, and does not say the opening supplication with his standing for the third unit. When he finishes the recitation of the chapter during it[349], he raises his hands parallel to his ears then he says "*Allāhu akbar*" and recites the *qunūt* standing before the bowing throughout the entire year. He does not recite the qunūt in other than the Witr prayer[350]. The meaning of qunūt is supplication. It is that he says:

*Allāhumma innā nastaᶜīnuka wa nastahdīk, wa nastaghfiruka wa natūbu ilayk, wa nu'minu bika wa natawakkalu ᶜalayk, wa nuthnī ᶜalaykal-khayra kullah, nashkuruka wa lā nakfuruk, wa nakhlaᶜu wa natruku man yafjuruk. Allāhumma iyyāka naᶜbudu wa laka nuṣallī wa nasjud, ilayka nasᶜā wa naḥfid, narjū raḥmatak wa nakhshā ᶜadhābak, inna ᶜadhābaka bil-kuffāri mulḥiq, wa ṣallallāhu ᶜalan-nabiyyi wa ālihi wa sallam.*[351]"

---

348 It has been narrated that it is sunnah and this is the opinion of Abu Yusuf and Muhammad [Maraqi al-Falah, page 216]. However, due to it being the most emphasised sunnah with them, they said that it must be made up if missed. See: [Bada'i al-Sana'i, Chapter of Witr].

349 The third unit [Maraqi al-Falah, page 217].

350 The qunūt is also permitted in the Fajr prayer if a calamity befalls the Muslims, it has also been said that it is permitted in the audible prayers and also said that it is permitted in all of the prayers. See: [Al-Lubab fi Sharh al-Kitab].

351 Oh Allah, we seek Your help, guidance, and forgiveness. We repent to You, believe in You, rely upon You, praise You for all good, thank You and are not ungrateful to

.........................................................................................................

.........................................................................................................

.........................................................................................................

.........................................................................................................

.........................................................................................................

.........................................................................................................

.........................................................................................................

The follower recites the qunūt just like the imam. If the imam begins the supplication *"Allāhummah-dinā"* to the end, after what preceded[352]; Abu Yusuf (may Allah have mercy upon him) said, "They follow him and recite with him." But Muhammad said, "They do not follow him, rather they say *āmīn*." It is this:

*Allāhummah-dinā bifaḍlika fīman hadayt, wa ʿāfinā fīman ʿāfayt, wa tawallanā fīman tawallayt, wa bārik lanā fīmā aʿṭayt, wa qinā sharra mā qaḍayt, innaka taqḍī wa la yuqḍā ʿalayk, innahu lā yadhillu man wālayt, wa lā yaʿizzu man ʿādayt, tabārakta rabbanā wa taʿālayt, wa ṣallallāhu ʿalā sayyidinā Muḥammadin wa ālihi wa ṣaḥbihi wa sallam.*[353]

Whoever has not perfected the qunūt says, "*Allāhumma-ghfirlī*[354]" three times or *"Rabbanā ātinā fid-dunyā ḥasanah, wa fil-ākhirati ḥasanah wa qinā ʿadhāban-nār*[355]*"* or *"Yā rabb, yā rabb, yā rabb.*[356]*"*

---

You, and we disown and abandon whoever disbelieves in You. Oh Allah, You alone we worship and to You we pray and prostrate. To You we strive and hasten, we hope for Your mercy and fear Your punishment, truly Your punishment is overtaking the disbelievers. May Allah send blessings and peace on the Prophet and his family.

352 The previous supplication mentioned.

353 Oh Allah guide us with those You have guided, grant us well-being with those You granted well-being, take charge of us with those You have taken charge of, bless us in what You have given us, and protect us from the evil that You have decreed, indeed you decree and cannot be decreed upon, indeed the one whom You showed allegiance to is never abased and the one whom You take as an enemy is never mighty. Oh our Lord, blessed and exalted are You, and may Allah send peace and blessings upon Muhmmad, his family, and his companions.

354 Oh Allah, forgive me.

355 Oh our Lord, grant us good in this world, good in the Hereafter, and save us from the punishment of the Hellfire."

356 Oh my Lord, oh my Lord, oh my Lord.

.......................................................................................................

.......................................................................................................

.......................................................................................................

.......................................................................................................

.......................................................................................................

.......................................................................................................

.......................................................................................................

If he prays behind someone who is reading the qunūt in the Fajr prayer, he stands quietly with him during his qunūt (according to the stronger view) and he releases his hands to his sides[357].

If he forgets the qunūt in the Witr prayer and remembers it during bowing or raising from it, he does not read the qunūt. If he reads the qunūt after raising his head from bowing, he does not repeat the bowing, but he prostrates for forgetfulness due to the disappearance of the qunūt from its original place.

If the imam bows before the follower's finishing of reading the qunūt or before his starting of it and he fears the missing of the bowing, he follows his imam.

If the imam leaves the qunūt, then the follower performs it if joining his imam in bowing is possible for him and if not, he follows him. If he catches the imam in the bowing of the third unit of the Witr prayer, he is someone who has caught the qunūt, therefore he does not perform it during what has preceded him[358].

Witr is performed in congregation in Ramadan only[359]. Its prayer with the congregation in Ramadan is superior than its performance alone at the end of the night in the chosen opinion of Qāḍī Khān[360], he said, "It is the correct opinion." Other than him have verified its opposite.

---

357 The same ruling applies if the qunūt is read in Witr after the bowing [Maraqi al-Falah, page 223].

358 i.e. When he stands to complete the units of prayer that he missed.

359 Imam Al-Ayni mentions that the correct opinion is that it is permitted due outside of Ramadan too to the sound hadith that Imam Al-Tahawi narrated in his Sharh Ma'ani al-Athar from Al-Miswar bin Makhramah who said, "We buried Abu Bakr at night and Umar said, 'I have not performed Al-Witr,' then he stood and we made rows behind him and he prayed three units without giving salutations except at the end of them" [Sharh Ma'ani al-Athar, 1742]. See: [Nukhab al-Afkar, Chapter of Al-Witr].

360 Al-Hasan bin Mansur bin Muhammad al-Awzjandi al-Farghani. One of the great imams of the Hanafi School and a student of Zahir al-Din al-Marghaynani and Ibrahim al-Saffar. He died on the 15th Ramadan 592AH, considered a mujtahid in scenarios.

............................................................................................................

............................................................................................................

............................................................................................................

............................................................................................................

............................................................................................................

## Section on Clarifying Voluntary[361] Prayers

Two units before the Fajr prayer, two after the Ẓuhr prayer, two after the maghrib prayer and after the ʿIshāʾ prayer, four before the Ẓuhr prayer, before[362] the Friday prayer and after it [363]with one salutation[364] have been made an emphasised sunnah.

Four before the ʿAṣr prayer, before al-ʿIshāʾ[365] and after it are recommended. Six after maghrib are recommended[366].

He restricts himself in the first sitting of a four-unit emphasised prayer to the tashahhud and does not perform the opening supplication in the third unit as opposed to the recommended prayer[367].

---

361 He mentions voluntary (*nawāfil*) and not sunnahs (*sunan*) because the voluntary (*nafl*) is more general since every sunnah is voluntary but not the opposite [Maraqi al-Falah, page 225].

362 Because the Prophet ﷺ would pray four before the Friday prayer without anything of a break in them [Maraqi al-Falah, page 226]. [Ibn Majah, 1129, in a very weak chain but declared authentic due to corroborating evidence *sahih lighayrihi* and Al-Tahawi in Sharh Ma'ani al-Athar, 1965, 1970 in a sound authentic chain].

363 All of the four-unit prayers.

364 Al-Zayla'i said, "If he prays them with two salutations, they would not be considered from the sunnah." [Maraqi al-Falah, page 227].

365 It has been said two before it are recommended [Al-Ikhtiyar, Chapter of Voluntary Prayers].

366 All of the traditions in relation to this are extremely weak or fabricated. See: [Al-Tirmidhi, 435; Ibn Majah, 1373; and Al-Tabarani in al-Awsat, 7245 and al-Saghir, 127/2].

367 This ruling has been criticised by the ulama of the school and has no basis in the Hadith. For a more detailed discussion, see: [Radd al-Muhtar, Section on Voluntary Prayers].

If he prays more than two units for a voluntary prayer and does not sit except at the end of it, it is valid due to *istiḥsān*[368] because it all became one prayer and it contains the obligation of the sitting at the end of it[369].

Increase of more than four units with one salutation during the day and eight during the night is disliked. Four is superior in both of them with Abu Hanifah and with Abu Yusuf and Muhammad sets of twos is superior during the night; fatwa is given with this. The prayer of the night is superior to the prayer of the day. Lengthy standing is superior to excessive prostration.

---

368 A type of ijtihad that entails leaving aside an apparent analogy for a subtle analogy. See: Preface.

369 The omission of the sitting after two units forgetfully is repaired with prostrating [Maraqi al-Falah, page 229]. i.e. By performing the prostration of forgetfulness at the end of the prayer.

## Section on Greeting the Mosque, the Forenoon Prayer, and Giving Life to Nights

Greeting the mosque with two units of prayer before sitting is sunnah. The performance of the farḍ prayer and every prayer that he performs when entering without the intention of greeting takes its place.

Two units of prayer are recommended after wudu before his becoming dry, four units and more in the forenoon, the night prayer, the decision-making prayer, and the prayer of need.

Giving life[370] to the last ten nights of Ramadan, the two nights of the two Eids[371], the ten nights of Dhul-Hijjah, the night of half of Sha'ban[372] is recommended.

---

370 By performing some act/acts of worship for the majority of the night.

371 I did not come across anything from Abu Hanifah or the early scholars menn tioning this, nor could I find any narration of the Prophet ﷺ or his companions (may Allah be pleased with them) singling them out as nights of worship. It was mentioned in a narration, "Whoever stands in prayer on the two nights of Eid, hoping of reward from Allah, his heart will not die on the day that hearts die." [Ibn Majah, 1782 and Al-Tabarani in al-Awsat, 159 with the wording: "Whoever prays on the night of (Eid) al-Fitr and the night of (Eid) al-Adha, his heart will not die on the day that hearts die." Al-Nawawi mentions the two chains of the hadith and then says, "Both of them are weak but laxity is applied with narrations mentioning virtuous actions." [Al-Adhkar, Chapter of Remembrances Legislated for the Two Eids). It was considered weak due to Baqiyyah bin al-Walid who narrates from liars and conceals faults (*tadlis*) in one chain and Umar bin Harun al-Balkhi in another who was accused of fabricating narrations in the other.

372 The fifteenth night. It was narrated that the Messenger of Allah ﷺ said: "Indeed

Gathering in the mosques for the purpose of giving life to any night from one of these nights is disliked[373].

Allah surely looks on the night of the fifteenth of *Shaᶜban* then forgives all of His creation except a polytheist or a schismatic innovator." [Ibn Majah, 1390; Al-Bayhaqi in Shu'ab al-Iman, 3833; Ibn Hibban, 5665; Al-Tabarani in al-Awsat, 6772; Ahmad, 6642; and Al-Bazzar, 2046. Hussayn al-Darani said, "The narrations are individually weak but authentic with all of their chains" in his footnotes on Majma' al-Zawa'id [Majma' al-Zawa'id, 12984-12989, Chapter of What Came Regarding Rancour, 190/16 Dar al-Minhaj]. Ibn Taymiyyah stated, "If a person prays the entire night on his own, or in a congregation, this is indeed something praiseworthy. However, as for praying a specific number of units of prayer in the mosque, such as one hundred units, while reciting Surah al-Ikhlas a thousand times, such actions are blameworthy innovations that none of the major scholars allowed." [Majmu al-Fatawa, 131-2/23].

373 And in any other place because the Prophet ﷺ did not do it, nor his companions [Maraqi al-Falah, page 235].

.........................................................................................................

.........................................................................................................

.........................................................................................................

.........................................................................................................

.........................................................................................................

## Section on the Voluntary Prayer Seated, the Prayer on a Riding-Beast, and the Prayer Walking

Voluntary prayer whilst seated with the ability to stand is permitted but he has half the reward of a standing person unless there is an excuse. He sits like the one performing the tashahhud according to the chosen opinion. His completing seated after his initiation standing is permitted without dislike according to the soundest opinion.

He can perform voluntary prayers whilst riding outside of the city[374], making indications in any direction that his riding-beast heads and he can build[375] with his alighting but not with his mounting even if it is with the orderly voluntary prayers[376]. It has been narrated from Abu Hanifah (may Allah have mercy upon him) that he should alight for the sunnahs of the Fajr prayer because they are more emphasised than the others.

It is permitted, without dislike, for the person performing voluntary prayers to lean against something if he becomes tired. It is disliked if it is without an excuse according to the stronger view due to bad manners.

An impurity on the riding-beast does not prevent the validity of the prayer, even if it is on the saddle and stirrups according to the soundest opinion.

The prayer of a walking person is not valid by consensus[377].

---

374 i.e. outside of the inhabited buildings in order to include the village and tents [Maraqi al-Falah, page 237].

375 Upon a prayer that he already initiated.

376 The emphasised ones [Maraqi al-Falah, page 238].

377 Consensus of our imams [Maraqi al-Falah, page 238].

.............................................................................................................

.............................................................................................................

.............................................................................................................

.............................................................................................................

.............................................................................................................

## Section on the Farḍ and Wājib Prayers Whilst on a Riding-beast

The farḍ prayers are not valid on a riding-beast, nor the wājib prayers such as the Witr prayer, a vowed prayer, or what he initiated as a voluntary prayer and ruined, nor the funeral prayer or a prostration that its verses were recited on the ground unless due to necessity such as fear for himself, his riding-beast, or clothing from a robber if he were to alight. Also, fear from a beast of prey, a muddy area, the recalcitrance of a riding-beast, and being unable to find someone to mount him due to his incapacity[378].

The prayer inside a carriage on a riding-beast is like the prayer on it whether it is moving or still. If he places a piece of wood under the carriage so that its stationariness to the ground remains, it takes the place of the ground, so the obligatory prayer is valid in it standing[379].

---

378 He does not need to repeat it when the excuse has gone [Maraqi al-Falah, page 239].

379 Not sitting [Maraqi al-Falah, page 239].

## Section on the Prayer in a Boat

The farḍ prayer is valid in it sitting with bowing and prostration without an excuse whilst it is sailing with Abu Hanifah. Abu Yusuf and Muhammad said that it is not valid unless there is an excuse and this is the stronger view. An excuse is such as dizziness and an inability to leave. Praying with indications in it is not permitted by agreement.

The boat that is anchored in the depth of the sea and is being moved by strong winds is like the moving boat, but if not[380], then it is like a stationary boat according to the soundest opinion. If it is anchored to the shore, then his prayer sitting is not permitted by consensus. So, if he prays standing and part of the boat is on the bottom of the ground, the prayer is valid and if not, then it is not valid according to the chosen opinion unless he is unable to exit.

The praying person faces the qiblah in it[381] at the opening of the prayer and every time it turns away from it[382], he turns towards it[383] during the prayer so that he completes it facing the qiblah.

---

380 If strong winds are not causing it to move [Maraqi al-Falah, page 240].

381 The boat.

382 The qiblah.

383 The qiblah.

## Section on Tarāwīḥ

The *tarāwīḥ*[384] are sunnah for men and women. Its prayer in congregation is a communal sunnah and its time is after the ʿIshā' prayer. The preceding of the Witr prayer before tarāwīḥ and delaying of it after them is valid. The delaying of tarāwīḥ to a third or half of the night is recommended and it is not disliked to delay it after it[385] according to the sound opinion.

They are twenty units with ten salutations. It is recommended to sit after every four by its amount, likewise between the fifth *tarwīḥah* and al-Witr.

Completion of the Quran in them once in the month is sunnah according to the sound opinion. However, if people become fed up with it, then he recites an amount that does not lead to their aversion according to the chosen opinion[386]. He does not leave the prayer on the Prophet ﷺ in every tashahhud of them even if people become fed up, according to the chosen opinion[387]. He does not leave the *thanā* and the glorifications of bowing and prostration.

384 Plural of *tarwīḥah* which is the sitting in between every four units of the night prayer performed in Ramadan. It was then used to mean the four units of prayer itself.
385 Half of the night [Maraqi al-Falah, page 240].
386 The best in our times is what does not lead to aversion of the congregation, this also in *Al-Ikhtiyar*. In *Al-Muhit*, "The best in our times is that he recites what does not lead to the aversion of people from the congregation because increasing the amount of people is better than lengthy recitation, and fatwa is given with this. Al-Zahidi said, "He recites as he recites in al-Maghrib i.e. with the short chapters after the fatihah." [Maraqi al-Falah, page 245].
387 He suffices with "Oh Allah send blessings on Muhammad" [Al-Durr al-Mukhtar, Section on Tarāwīḥ].

.........................................................................................................

.........................................................................................................

.........................................................................................................

.........................................................................................................

.........................................................................................................

.........................................................................................................

.........................................................................................................

However, he does not perform the supplication if people become fed up[388].

Tarāwīḥ are not made up alone nor in congregation due to missing them.

---

388 He does not leave it completely but supplicates with what is short in order to obtain the sunnah [Maraqi al-Falah, page 245].

..........................................................................................

..........................................................................................

..........................................................................................

..........................................................................................

..........................................................................................

..........................................................................................

..........................................................................................

## Section of Prayer Inside the Kaaba

The farḍ and voluntary prayer is valid in it. Likewise, on top of it, even if he does not use a barrier, but it is disliked due to bad etiquette of his elevation above it. Whoever places his back, whilst in it or on top of it, in other than the face of his imam, it is valid[389]. If he places his back towards the face of his imam, it is not valid.

His following outside of it of an imam inside of it whilst the door is open is valid.

If they make a circle around it and the imam is outside of it, it[390] is valid except for the one who is closer to it in the direction of his imam.

389 His following of him [Maraqi al-Falah, page 246].

390 The following of all of them [Maraqi al-Falah, page 247].

.......................................................................................................

.......................................................................................................

.......................................................................................................

.......................................................................................................

.......................................................................................................

.......................................................................................................

.......................................................................................................

## Section of the Traveller's Prayer

The least amount of travel that legal rulings change with is the distance of three days from the shortest days of the year at average pace[391] with breaks. 'Average' is the pace of camels and walking on land.[392] On a mountain, it is what is appropriate for it[393]. In the sea, it is with moderate wind.

Whoever intends travel, even if he is disobedient by his travel, and passes the houses of his place of residence and also passes what is connected to its[394] open space, shortens the four-unit farḍ. However, if the open space is separated by a farm or the amount of a *ghalwah*[395], then passing it is not a condition. The open space is a place prepared for the benefits of the city such as the running of riding-beasts and burying of the deceased.

---

391 During the daytime because the night is not a realm for travelling, rather it is for resting [Maraqi al-Falah, page 249].

392 It has been estimated by some as 15 *farsakh*, some others as 18 *farsakh*, and others as 21 *farsakh*. [Al-Muhit al-Burhani, Chapter of the Traveller's Prayer]. The *farsakh* is the *parasang*, a historical Iranian unit of itinerant distance, the length of which varied according to terrain and speed of travel. The European equivalent is the "*league*". It has been estimated as approximately 3 miles, a mile being 4,000 arm-lengths which are approximately 46cm in length each. See: [Hashiyah al-Tahtawi, Chapter of Tayammum].

393 Because there is elevation, depression, flat terrain, and rugged terrain. Thereefore, travel by camel and walking will be less than their pace on flat ground [Maraqi al-Falah, page 249].

394 His place of residence [Maraqi al-Falah, page 250].

395 300-400 feet.

.......................................................................................................

.......................................................................................................

.......................................................................................................

.......................................................................................................

.......................................................................................................

.......................................................................................................

.......................................................................................................

Three things are a condition for the validity of the intention for travel:

1. Independence with the ruling.
2. Puberty.
3. The length of travel not being shorter than three days[396].

Therefore, the one who has not passed the houses of his place of residence, or passes as a child, or as follower and his leader did not intend travel such as a woman with her husband, a slave with his master, and a soldier with his commander, or he intends less than three, does not shorten the prayer.

The intention of residency and travel is considered from the origin[397] not the follower if the follower knows the intention of the leader according to the soundest opinion[398].

Shortening is an original ruling[399] with us[400], so if he completes four units and sat for the first sitting, his prayer is valid with dislike[401] and if not, then it is not valid unless he intended residency when he stood up for the third unit. He continues to shorten until he enters his city or he intends his residency for half a month in a city or village. He shortens if he intends less than that or he does not intend and remains for years.

---

396 Meaning the distance of three days as mentioned previously.

397 Such as the husband, master, and commander [Maraqi al-Falah, page 251].

398 Therefore, until the follower knows about the intention of residency from the leader, they do not have to complete the full prayer [Maraqi al-Falah, page 251].

399 ʿ*Azīmah* as opposed to being a dispensation (*ruksah*). Meaning that it is the default ruling.

400 The Hanafis.

401 For delaying a wājib act i.e. the salutation from its place if he did it intentionally, but if he did it forgetfully, then he prostrates for forgetfulness [Maraqi al-Falah, page 251].

.......................................................................................................................

.......................................................................................................................

.......................................................................................................................

.......................................................................................................................

.......................................................................................................................

.......................................................................................................................

.......................................................................................................................

Intention of residency in two cities that he did not specify staying overnight in one of them is not valid. Nor is it valid in the desert for other than tent dwellers, nor for our[402] military in non-Muslim lands, nor in our lands when laying siege to rebels.

If a traveller follows[403] the resident in the prayer time then it is valid and he completes four units. However, after the time[404] it is not valid but the opposite way[405] around it is valid in both scenarios[406]. It is recommended for the imam to say, "Complete your prayer because I am travelling." He should say this before his initiation of the prayer. The resident does not recite during what he completes after the finishing of his traveller imam according to the soundest opinion.

The missed prayer of travel and home residence is made up as two units and four units. The consideration in this is with the end of the prayer time.

An original abode is only annulled with what is similar to it. An abode of residence is annulled with what is similar to it, with travel, and with[407] the original.

An original abode is that which he was born in, married in, or did not get married but intended to make a living and not move from it.

---

402 The Muslims.

403 Praying four units, even in the final sitting [Maraqi al-Falah, page 253].

404 After the exiting of the prayer time [Maraqi al-Falah, page 253].

405 With the traveller leading the prayer.

406 In the prayer time and after it. The reason is that the sitting of the traveller is farḍ and his two units do not change after the prayer time exits, so his sitting will be stronger than the sitting of the resident whose first sitting is only wājib.

407 Returning back to his original abode.

........................................................................................................

........................................................................................................

........................................................................................................

........................................................................................................

........................................................................................................

........................................................................................................

........................................................................................................

An abode of residence is a place that he intended residency in for half a month or more. The *Verifiers*[408] did not consider the abode of sojourn which is what he intended residency in for less than half a month[409].

---

408 Scholars who researched and verified the soundness of legal rulings in the school.

409 Therefore, the abode of residence will not be annulled by it [Maraqi al-Falah, page 254].

.................................................................................................................

.................................................................................................................

.................................................................................................................

.................................................................................................................

.................................................................................................................

.................................................................................................................

.................................................................................................................

.................................................................................................................

## Section of the Sick Person's Prayer

If all the standing is impossible or becomes difficult for the sick person due to the presence of severe pain, fear of an increase in the illness, or a delay in it because of standing, then he prays seated with bowing and prostration and he sits however he wants according to the soundest opinion. If not[410], then he stands for the amount that he is able to. If bowing and prostration is impossible, then he prays seated with indications. He makes his indication[411] for prostration lower than his indication[412] for bowing. If he does not make it lower than it, then the prayer is not valid. He does not raise something to his face to prostrate on. However, if he does and lowers his head[413], then it is valid and if not, then no.

If sitting is impossible, he makes indications lying down or on his side but the former is more appropriate. He places a pillow under his head so that his face ends up towards the qiblah not the sky. He should erect his knees if able to so that he does not stretch them towards the qiblah.

---

410 By him being able to stand for a part of it [Maraqi al-Falah, page 255].

411 With his head [Maraqi al-Falah, page 255].

412 With his head [Maraqi al-Falah, page 255].

413 For prostration lower than his indication for his bowing [Maraqi al-Falah, page 256].

........................................................................................................

........................................................................................................

........................................................................................................

........................................................................................................

........................................................................................................

........................................................................................................

........................................................................................................

........................................................................................................

If indications[414] are impossible, then it[415] is delayed for him as long as he understands the divine address. He[416] said in *Al-Hidāyah*, "It is the sound opinion," however, the author of *Al-Hidāyah* asserted with certainty in *Al-Tajnīs wa al-Mazīd* the omission of making up if his inability to make indications is for more than five prayers even if he understands the divine address. Qāḍī Khān[417] considered it as sound, similar to it is in *Al-Muḥīṭ*, and Shaykh al-Islam[418] and Fakhr al-Islam[419] chose it. He said[420] in *Al-Ẓahīriyyah*, "It is *Ẓāhir al-Riwāyah* and the fatwa is given on it." In *Al-Khulāṣah*, "It is the chosen opinion." He considered it sound in *Al-Yanābīᶜ*[421] and in *Al-Badāᶜi*, and Al-Walwājī[422] asserted it with certainty (may Allah have mercy on them).

He does not make indications with his eyes, heart, or eyebrows.

If he is able to stand but is incapable of bowing and prostrating, he prays seated with indications.

---

414 With his head [Maraqi al-Falah, page 257].

415 A small amount of prayers which is the prayers of a day and night or less [Maraqi al-Falah, page 257].

416 Imam Abu al-Hasan Ali al-Marghaynani. Died on the 14th of Dhul-Hijjah, 593AH.

417 Al-Hasan bin Mansur bin Muhammad al-Awzjandi al-Farghani. One of the great imams of the Hanafi School and a student of Zahir al-Din al-Marghaynani and Ibrahim al-Saffar. He died on the 15th Ramadan 592AH, considered a mujtahid in scenarios.

418 Imam Muhammad bin Husayn al-Bukhari aka Bakr Khuwaharzadah. Died in Bukhara on Friday 25th Jumada al-Ula, 483AH.

419 Imam Ali bin Muhammad al-Bazdawi. Imam of his time in practical rulings and principles. Died 482AH.

420 Al-Qadi Zahir al-Din al-Bukhari. Died 619AH.

421 *Al-Yanābīᶜ fi Maᶜrifah al-Uṣūl wa al-Tafārīᶜ* either authored by Rashid al-Din al-Rumi, died: 769AH or Badr al-Din al-Shibli, died: 769AH.

422 Zahir al-Din Ishaq bin Abu Bakr. Walwaj is a city in the Badakhshan Province (now northeastern Afghanistan). Died 467AH.

If an illness overcomes him, he completes it with whatever he is capable of, even if with indications according to the well-known opinion. If he prays seated bowing and prostrating, then becomes well, he builds. However, if he was making indications, no.

Whoever loses sanity or becomes unconscious for the duration of five prayers makes them up, but if more, no.

## Section on Omission of Prayer and Fasting and Other Than These Two

If a sick person dies and was unable to perform the prayer with indications, it is not obligatory for him to make a bequest for them[423] even if they are few[424]. The same is for fasting if the traveller or sick person breaks the fast and dies before residency and health.

He must make a bequest for what he was able to do and remained in his responsibility. Therefore, his guardian will take out half a *ṣāʿ*[425] of wheat or its value on his behalf from a third of what he left for the fast of every day and for the prayer of every time, even the Witr prayer. If he never made a bequest and his guardian donates on his behalf, it is valid.

It is not valid to fast or pray on his behalf.

If what he bequeathed does not fulfil what is binding upon him, that amount is paid to a poor person and thus it will be omitted from him according to its amount. Then the poor person gifts it to the guardian and he takes possession of it then pays it to the poor person and so on until whatever prayers and fasts were binding on the deceased are omitted. Giving the compensation for numerous prayers to one person in one go is permitted as opposed to expiation of an oath. Allah ﷻ knows best.

423 The prayers.

424 With them being short of twenty-four hours of prayers due to what I narrated because of his inability to make them up by reaching a new time [Maraqi al-Falah, page 260].

425 An archaic measure of volume equivalent to approximately 3 litres or less.

### Section of Making Up Missed Prayers

Maintaining the order between a missed prayer and a prayer of the time and between the missed prayers is obligatory (*mustaḥaqq*). It is omitted with one of three things:

1. Constriction of the recommended time according to the soundest opinion.
2. Forgetfulness.
3. If the missed prayers become six excluding the Witr prayer because it is not counted as an omitter even if its order[426] is binding.

The order does not return with their returning to a small number nor with the missing of a new prayer after six old prayers according to the soundest opinion in these two scenarios. Thus, if he prayed a farḍ whilst remembering a missed prayer, even a Witr prayer, then his farḍ is ruined as a suspended ruining. So if the time of the fifth prayer exited from what he prayed after the missed prayer whilst remembering it, then all of them are valid[427] therefore they won't be invalid by making up the missed prayer after it[428]. However, if he makes up the missed prayer before the exiting of the time of the fifth prayer, the attribute[429] of what he prayed whilst remembering before them is invalid and they become voluntary (*nafl*)[430].

---

426 With al-ʿIshāʾ and al-Fajr [Maraqi al-Falah, page 265].
427 With Abu Hanifah [Maraqi al-Falah, page 265].
428 After the exiting of the time of the fifth prayer [Maraqi al-Falah, page 266].
429 Not the prayer in and of itself though.
430 With Abu Hanifah and Abu Yusuf [Maraqi al-Falah, page 266]. Although it

If the missed prayers become a lot, then specifying of each prayer is needed. If he wants to make the matter easy, then he can intend the first Ẓuhr prayer binding upon him or the last one. The same is for fasting from two Ramadans according to one of the two differing verified opinions.

The one who converts to Islam in non-Muslim lands is excused of his ignorance of legal rulings.

---

should be noted that it is prohibited for him to delay making up the missed prayer without an excuse.

..............................................................................................................

..............................................................................................................

..............................................................................................................

..............................................................................................................

..............................................................................................................

..............................................................................................................

..............................................................................................................

## Section of Catching the Obligatory Prayer with the Imam

If he begins a farḍ prayer alone and the congregation is established, he breaks out of it[431] and follows if he did not prostrate for what he began or he prostrated in a non-four-unit prayer. If he prostrated in a four-unit prayer, he adds a second unit, gives salutations (so that the two units will become a voluntary prayer for him), and then follows praying the farḍ prayer. However, if he prayed three units, he completes it[432] and then follows praying a voluntary prayer[433] except at ʿAṣr time. If he stands up for the third unit and it is established before his prostration, he breaks out of it standing with one salutation according to the soundest opinion.

If he is in the sunnah of the Friday prayer and the one giving the sermon comes out or he is in the sunnah of the Ẓuhr prayer and it is established, he gives salutations at the end of two units; it is the most considerable opinion, then he makes up his sunnah after the farḍ prayer.

Whoever arrives and the imam is in the farḍ prayer, follows him and does not busy himself from it with the sunnah except in the Fajr prayer if he feels safe from missing it. However, if he does not feel safe, then he leaves it[434]. The sunnah of the Fajr prayer is not made up except when it is missed with the farḍ. He makes up the sunnah that is before the Ẓuhr prayer in its time before its two units[435]. He has not prayed Ẓuhr in congregation by him catching one

---

431 With one salutation whilst standing [Maraqi al-Falah, page 268].

432 As four units [Maraqi al-Falah, page 268].

433 If he wants [Maraqi al-Falah, page 268].

434 The sunnah.

435 i.e. The two sunnah after it.

unit, rather he has attained its virtue and it was differed upon about the one who catches three units.

He performs voluntary prayer before the farḍ if he feels safe from missing the time and if not, then no.

Whoever catches his imam in the bowing position, then does the opening takbīr and stands until the imam raises his head, has not caught the unit. If he bows before his imam after the imam's recitation of what the prayer would be permitted with[436], it is valid[437]and if not, no.

His leaving a mosque after the adhan has been called in it is disliked until he prays unless he is going to establish another congregation[438]. If he leaves after his prayer alone, it is not disliked unless the congregation was established for the Ẓuhr and ʿIshā' prayers before his leaving. Thus, he follows in both of them making a voluntary prayer.

After a prayer, he does not pray one similar to it.

---

436 Which is one verse [Maraqi al-Falah, page 272].

437 His bowing [Maraqi al-Falah, page 272].

438 Like the imam or caller to prayer of a different mosque [Maraqi al-Falah, page 273].

## Section of Prostrating due to Forgetfulness

Two prostrations with a tashahhud and salutations are wājib for the omission of a wājib act forgetfully[439] even if it is repeated. If his omission of it was intentional, he is sinful and repetition of the prayer is wājib in order to repair its deficiency.
He does not prostrate for forgetfulness for the intentional, it was said, "Except in three[440]:

1. Omitting the first sitting or,
2. his delaying a prostration from the first unit until the end of the prayer and
3. his pondering intentionally inasmuch as it occupies him from[441] a pillar."

It is sunnah to perform the prostrating due to forgetfulness after the salutations and one salutation to his right is sufficient according to the soundest opinion. If he prostrates before the salutations it is mildly disliked.

Prostrating due to forgetfulness is omitted with the rising of the sun after the salutations in the Fajr prayer, with its redness in the ʿAṣr prayer, and with the presence of what prevents building[442] after the salutations.

---

439 By preceding, delay, increase, or decrease but not for a sunnah [Maraqi al-Falah, page 274].
440 Scenarios.
441 The amount [Maraqi al-Falah, page 275].
442 On the prayer.

The follower must prostrate due to the forgetfulness of his imam, not his forgetfulness. The latecomer prostrates with his imam and then stands to make up what he was preceded with. If the latecomer forgets during what he is making up, he prostrates for it as well, but not the one who started the prayer with the imam.

The imam does not perform the prostrating due to forgetfulness in the Friday prayer and the two Eid prayers.

Whoever forgets the first sitting from the farḍ prayer goes back to it as long as he does not stand up straight according to *Ẓāhir al-Riwāyah* and it is the soundest opinion. The follower is like the one praying voluntary prayer, he goes back even if he completed standing. If he goes back and he is closer to standing, he prostrates due to forgetfulness and if he is closer to sitting, no prostrating is necessary for him according to the soundest opinion. If he goes back after he completed standing the sound opinion was differed upon regarding the ruining of his prayer[443].

If he forgets the final sitting, he goes back as long as he does not prostrate and then he prostrates[444] for his delaying the farḍ of sitting. However, if he prostrated, his farḍ becomes a voluntary prayer and he adds a sixth unit if he wishes even in the ʿAṣr prayer and a fourth unit in the Fajr prayer.

There is no dislike in adding to both of them[445] according to the sound opinion and he does not prostrate due to forgetfulness according to the soundest opinion. If he sits for the final sitting, then stands, he goes back and gives salutations[446] without repeating the tashahhud. If he prostrates, his farḍ is

443 The stronger of the two is that it is not ruined [Maraqi al-Falah, page 277].
444 For forgetfulness.
445 The Fajr prayer and the Maghrib prayer [Maraqi al-Falah, page 278].
446 If he gives salutations standing, it is valid [Maraqi al-Falah, page 278].

not ruined and he adds another unit[447] to it in order for the two extra units to become a voluntary prayer and he prostrates due to forgetfulness.

If he prostates due to forgetfulness in two units of voluntary prayer, he does not build two more units upon them as a recommendation. If he does build, then he repeats the prostrating due to forgetfulness according to the chosen opinion.

If the one who has a prostrating due to forgetfulness gives salutations and then someone follows him, it is valid[448] if he prostrates[449] due to forgetfulness and if not, it is not valid.

He prostrates due to forgetfulness even if he gave salutations intentionally for discontinuation as long as he has not turned away from the qiblah or speaks.

A person praying four or three units imagined that he completed them and gave salutations then realised that he prayed two units completes them and prostrates due to forgetfulness. If his pondering becomes lengthy and he does not give salutations so that he can ascertain certainty; if it is the amount of the performance of a pillar, prostrating due to forgetfulness is wājib upon him and if not[450], no.

---

447 As a recommendation [Maraqi al-Falah, page 278].

448 The following.

449 The one who forgot [Maraqi al-Falah, page 279].

450 If his pondering is not the amount of the performance of a pillar [Maraqi al-Falah, page 280].

## Section on Doubt in the Prayer and Purification

The prayer becomes invalid with doubt concerning the number of its units if it is before its completion and it is the first time that doubt has occurred to him or doubt is not habitual for him[451].

If he doubted after his salutations, it is not considered unless he becomes certain of omission.

If the doubt is frequent, he[452] works with his strong belief. If belief is not strong for him, he goes with the least and sits after every unit that he believes to be the end of his prayer.

451 That it happens more than once in a year [Hashiyah al-Tahtawi, Section on Doubt in the Prayer and Purification].
452 investigates and [Maraqi al-Falah, page 281].

## Section of Prostrating due to Recitation

Its cause is recitation to the reciter and the listener according to the sound opinion. It is wājib with a delay if it is not in the prayer. It is mildly disliked to delay it. It is wājib upon whoever recites a verse, even in Persian. Recitation of a word of the prostration with a word before it or after it from its verses is like the verse[453] according to the sound opinion.

Its verses are fourteen verses:

1. In Al-Aʿrāf[454],
2. in Al-Raʿd[455],
3. Al-Naḥl[456],
4. Al-Isrā'[457],
5. Maryam[458],
6. Al-Ḥajj[459],
7. Al-Furqān[460],

---

453 It necessitates prostrating [Maraqi al-Falah, page 283].
454 7:206.
455 13:15.
456 16:50.
457 Also known as *Banī Isrāīl*, 17:109.
458 19:58.
459 22:18.
460 25:60.

..........

..........

..........

..........

..........

..........

..........

8. Al-Naml[461],

9. Al-Sajdah[462],

10. Ṣād[463],

11. Ḥā-Mīm Sajdah[464],

12. Al-Najm[465],

13. Inshaqqat[466], and

14. Iqra'[467].

Prostrating is wājib upon whoever hears it, even if he did not intend to listen, apart from the menstruating woman, the woman in postpartum bleeding, and the imam and the one following him due to hearing it from a follower[468]. If they[469] hear it from someone else[470], they prostrate after the prayer and if they prostrate in the prayer, it will not suffice them, however, their prayer is not ruined according to *Ẓāhir al-Riwāyah*.

It is wājib by hearing it in Persian if he understands it according to the reliable opinion. The sound opinion was differed upon regarding it being wājib due to the hearing of it from a sleeping or insane person. It is not wājib due to hearing it from a bird and echoing.

---

461 27:26.
462 32:15.
463 38:24-25.
464 Also known as *Fuṣṣilat*, 41:28.
465 53:62.
466 Also known as *Al-Inshiqāq*, 84:21.
467 Also known as *Al-ᶜAlaq*, 96:19.
468 Of the imam that heard it or another imam [Maraqi al-Falah, page 286].
469 The followers and the imam [Maraqi al-Falah, page 286].
470 Other than the follower [Maraqi al-Falah, page 286].

.......................................................................................................

.......................................................................................................

.......................................................................................................

.......................................................................................................

.......................................................................................................

.......................................................................................................

.......................................................................................................

It is performed with bowing or prostrating in the prayer, other than the bowing of the prayer and its prostrating. The bowing of the prayer compensates it[471] if he intends it and also its[472] prostration even if he does not intend it as long as he does not interrupt the immediacy of the recitation by more than two verses.

If he hears it from an imam and does not join the prayer behind him or he joins the prayer behind him in another unit, he prostrates outside of the prayer according to the stronger view. If he joins the prayer behind him before the prostrating of his imam for it, he prostrates with him. If he follows him[473] in its unit after the prostration for it, he becomes someone who has caught it[474] legally, therefore, he does not perform its prostration whatsoever.

The prostration due to recitation done in the prayer is not made up outside of it. If he recited outside of the prayer, then prostrated, then repeated it[475] in it[476], he prostrates another prostration. If he did not prostrate initially, one prostration suffices him according to *Ẓāhir al-Riwāyah*, just like the one who repeats it in one gathering but not two gatherings.

The gathering changes due to moving from it, even if he is weaving the warp of a garment[477]. Also, by moving from branch to branch and swimming in a river or large pool according to the soundest opinion. It is not changed with the corners of a house[478], nor with the mosque, even if it is large, nor with the

471 The prostrating due to recitation.
472 The prayer's.
473 The imam.
474 The prostration.
475 The recitation of the verse.
476 The prayer.
477 By him going with the warp in his hand and throwing it on sticks erected in a wall and the ground [Maraqi al-Falah, page 290].
478 A small one [Maraqi al-Falah, page 290].

movement of a ship, nor with a unit of prayer[479] or two units, nor a drink or eating two morsels, nor walking two paces[480], nor with leaning against something, nor sitting, nor standing, nor mounting or descending in the place of his recitation, nor by the movement of his riding-beast whilst he is praying. The obligation upon the listener is repeated due to a change of his gathering and the gathering of the reciter is one but not with its opposite[481] according to the soundest opinion.

It is disliked for him to recite a chapter and omit the verse of prostration but not the opposite of it. It is recommended to add a verse or more to it[482]. It is recommended to conceal it from the one who is not prepared for it. It is recommended to stand then to prostrate for it and[483] the listener does not raise his head from it before the reciter of it. The reciter is not ordered to go forward, nor the listeners with making rows, hence, they prostrate however they are.

The conditions of the prayer have been made conditional for its validity apart from the taḥrīmah.

Its method is that he prostrates a single prostration between two takbīrs (which are two sunnahs) without raising a hand, tashahhud, or salutations.

---

479 That the recitation has been repeated in [Maraqi al-Falah, page 290].
480 In the desert [Maraqi al-Falah, page 291].
481 That the gathering of the listener is one [Maraqi al-Falah, page 291].
482 To repel the idea of preference [Maraqi al-Falah, page 291].
483 It is recommended [Maraqi al-Falah, page 291].

........................................................................................................................

........................................................................................................................

........................................................................................................................

........................................................................................................................

........................................................................................................................

........................................................................................................................

........................................................................................................................

........................................................................................................................

## Section on the Prostration of Gratitude

The prostration of gratitude is disliked with Imam Abu Hanifah (May Allah have mercy upon him). They both said[484], "It is an act of worship that is rewarded for." Its form is like the prostration of recitation.

Imam al-Nasafi[485] said in *Al-Kāfī*[486], "Whoever recites the verses of prostration entirely in one gathering and prostrates for every one of them, Allah will take care of that which distress him."[487]

484 Muhammad and also Abu Yusuf in one of the narrations from him [Maraqi al-Falah, page 293].

485 Abdullah bin Ahmad bin Mahmud [Maraqi al-Falah, page 293]. Abul Barakat, died 710AH in Baghdad.

486 Al-Kafi Sharh al-Wafi.

487 Imam al-Nasafi mentioned, "It has been said that whoever recites..." without any chain of transmission! However, there is no basis for it in any prophetic narrations.

........................................................................................................................

........................................................................................................................

........................................................................................................................

........................................................................................................................

........................................................................................................................

........................................................................................................................

........................................................................................................................

........................................................................................................................

## Section of the Friday Prayer

The Friday prayer is an individual farḍ upon the one who seven conditions are gathered in:

1. Masculinity.
2. Freedom.
3. Residency in a metropolis (*miṣr*[488]) or what is considered in the

488 The opinions regarding the definition of a metropolis (*miṣr jāmiᶜ*) is varied. Al-Karkhi mentioned that it is where penal punishments are established and legal rulings implemented. There are numerous narrations from Abu Yusuf; he mentioned in *Al-Imla,* "Every place that has a ruler and a judge to implement legal rulings and establish penal punishments is a miṣr and the Friday prayer is obligatory for its people." In another narration he said, "If the people in a town who one mosque is not enough for them gather, the head of state builds a grand mosque and appoints someone to pray the Friday prayer with them." In another narration, "If there are ten thousand or more in a town, I would order them to establish the Friday prayer in it." Some of our companions said, "The metropolis is where every tradesman can make a living with his trade from year to year without needing to switch to another trade." It was transmitted from Abu Abdullah al-Balkhi that he said, "The best thing said about it, is that it is when they gather in its largest of mosques, that it would not be able to contain them inasmuch as that they would need to build a Friday mosque, then this is a metropolis that Friday prayer is established in." Sufyan al-Thawri said, "The metropolis is what people consider to be a metropolis when unrestricted metropolises are mentioned." Abul Qasim al-Saffar was asked about the definition of a metropolis where the Friday prayer would be valid and he said, "That they have

..........................................................................................................

..........................................................................................................

..........................................................................................................

..........................................................................................................

..........................................................................................................

..........................................................................................................

..........................................................................................................

..........................................................................................................

limit of residency[489] in it according to the soundest opinion.

4. Health.
5. Safety from an oppressor.
6. Soundness of the eyes[490].
7. Soundness of the legs.

Six things are conditional for its validity:

1. The metropolis or its open space[491].

---

defensive force to the point that if an enemy came to them, they would be able to defend it. In that case, it is valid for it to be made a metropolis which is that an upright governor is appointed to implement a legal ruling from legal rulings which is that two opponents come forward to him and he judges between them." It was narrated from Abu Hanifah that it is a large city that has streets, markets, and districts and it has a governor that is able to exact justice for the oppressed from the oppressor with his entourage, knowledge, or someone else's knowledge and people refer to him in relation to incidents. This is the soundest opinion. [Bada'i al-Sana'i, Section on the Conditions of the Friday Prayer, 2/192].

489 Leaving the metropolis also permits the omission of the of the Friday prayer, Eid prayers, congregational prayer, and permits praying voluntary prayers on a riding-beast, and performing tayammum, and causes the recommendation of choosing lots between his wives. See: [Hashiyah al-Tahtawi, Chapter of the Traveller's Prayer] and [Al-Ashbah wa al-Naza'ir, Rule Number Four].

490 Thus, it is not obligatory upon a blind person with Abu Hanifah as opposed to Abu Yusuf and Muhammad if he finds a guide to take him [Maraqi al-Falah, page 296].

491 That is not separated from it by more than a *ghalwah* (approximately 400 yards) [Maraqi al-Falah, page 296].

........................................................................................................

........................................................................................................

........................................................................................................

........................................................................................................

........................................................................................................

........................................................................................................

........................................................................................................

........................................................................................................

2. The head of state or his deputy[492].

3. The time of Ẓuhr, so it is not valid before it and becomes invalid with its exiting.

4. The sermon[493] before it with intention of it in its time and the presence of someone that the Friday prayer can be conducted with to hear it, even one person according to the sound opinion.

5. Universal permission[494].

6. The congregation. They are three men other than the imam even if they are slaves, travellers, or sick people. The condition is that they remain with the imam until he prostrates. If they run away after his prostrating, he finishes it alone as the Friday prayer and if they run away before his prostrating, it is invalid. It is not valid with a woman or a child with two men.

It is permitted for the slave and the sick person[495] to lead it.

The metropolis (miṣr) is every place that has a mufti, a ruler, and a judge[496] to implement legal rulings and establish penal punishments and its buildings have reached the amount of buildings at Mina according to *Ẓāhir al-Riwāyah*.

---

492 i.e. His command to establish the Friday prayer [Maraqi al-Falah, page 297]. If non-Muslim rulers conquer Muslims, then it is permitted for the Muslims to establish Friday and Eid prayers and a judge will become a judge by mutual consent of the Muslims [Hashiyah al-Tahtawi, Chapter of the Friday Prayer].

493 Even in Persian from one who has the ability to speak Arabic [Maraqi al-Falah, page 297].

494 Because it is from the symbols of Islam and the idiosyncrasies of the religion, so it must be established in a universal and publicised way [Maraqi al-Falah, page 298].

495 And the traveller [Maraqi al-Falah, page 299].

496 That are all resident in it [Maraqi al-Falah, page 299].

If the judge or the ruler is a mufti, then it suffices the need for diversity[497]. The Friday prayer at Mina is valid during the pilgrimage season for the head of state or the governor of the *Ḥijāz*[498].

It is valid to restrict the sermon to something like one *tasbīḥah*[499] or *taḥmīdah*[500] with dislike[501]. The sunnahs of the sermon are eighteen things:

1. Purification.
2. Covering nakedness.
3. Sitting on the mimbar before initiating the sermon.
4. The adhan in front of him just like the iqāmah,
5. then his standing.
6. A sword in his left hand, resting upon it, in every land that was conquered forcefully and without it in every land that was conquered by settlement.
7. Facing the people with his face.
8. His beginning with praise of Allah and commendation of Him with what He deserves.
9. The two testifications (*al-shahādatān*).
10. Sending blessings upon the Prophet ﷺ.

497 Because it revolves around knowledge of the legal rulings not the number of people [Maraqi al-Falah, page 299].
498 The western region of present-day Saudi Arabia.
499 An utterance of glorification.
500 An utterance of praise.
501 For leaving the sunnah [Maraqi al-Falah, page 299].

11. Giving admonition and reminding.
12. Recitation of one verse of the Quran.
13. Two sermons.
14. Sitting between the two sermons.
15. Repeating the praise, commendation, and blessings upon the Prophet ﷺ at the beginning of the second sermon and
16. supplication for the believing men and women by asking forgiveness for them.
17. That he makes people hear the sermon.
18. Shortening the two sermons to the length of a chapter from the lengthy separated chapters.

Lengthening and leaving something from the sunnahs is disliked.

Heading to the Friday prayer and leaving trade is obligatory at the first adhan according to the soundest opinion.

If the imam comes out, then there is no prayer, no speech, he does not return salutations nor respond to a sneezing person until he[502] finishes his prayer. Eating, drinking, playing around, and turning around are disliked for the one who is attending the sermon. The one giving the sermon does not give salutations to the people when he mounts the mimbar.

Leaving the metropolis after the call is disliked until he prays. If the one who the Friday prayer is not obligatory for performs it, it compensates for the obligatory prayer of the time. If the person who has no excuse prays the Ẓuhr

---

502 The imam.

........................................................................................................

........................................................................................................

........................................................................................................

........................................................................................................

........................................................................................................

........................................................................................................

........................................................................................................

........................................................................................................

prayer before it[503], it is prohibited. If he heads to it and the imam is in it, his Ẓuhr prayer is invalid even if he does not catch it.

It is disliked for the one who is excused and the prisoner to perform the Ẓuhr prayer in congregation in the metropolis on its day.

Whoever catches it in the tashahhud or the prostrating due to forgetfulness, he completes the Friday prayer.

---

503 Before the Friday prayer [Maraqi al-Falah, page 303].

........................................................................................................................

........................................................................................................................

........................................................................................................................

........................................................................................................................

........................................................................................................................

........................................................................................................................

........................................................................................................................

........................................................................................................................

## Section of the Rulings of the Two Eids

The prayer of the two Eids is wājib upon whoever the Friday prayer is obligatory upon with its conditions except for the sermon. Thus, it is valid without it but with *isā'ah*[504] just as if the sermon was done before the prayer.
Thirteen things are recommended for *al-Fiṭr*[505]:

1. That he eats[506].
2. That the food eaten is dates.
3. And they are an odd number.
4. That he performs ghusl.
5. That he brushes his teeth.
6. That he wears fragrance[507].
7. That he wears his best clothing.
8. That he fulfils the charity of al-Fiṭr if it is obligatory upon him.
9. That he expresses joy and happiness.
10. Abundant charity according to his ability.

---

504 For leaving the sunnah [Maraqi al-Falah, page 305]. This is a general term to indicate an action that is contrary to the sunnah and varies in its severity according to the action.
505 The Eid celebrated after Ramadan.
506 After the Fajr prayer, before going to the prayer area.
507 Even from his wife's perfume [Maraqi al-Falah, page 306].

11. Earliness, which is to awaken quickly.
12. Arriving early.
13. The dawn prayer in his local mosque.

Then he heads to the prayer area walking, saying the takbīr silently. He ends it when he arrives at the prayer area according to one narration and in another, when he begins the prayer. He returns using a different route.

It is disliked to perform voluntary prayer in the prayer area or at home before the Eid prayer and after it in the prayer area only according to the chosen position of the majority.

The time of validity for the Eid prayer is from the elevation of the sun the amount of a spear or two spears[508] up until its movement from the zenith.

The method of the two Eid prayers is that he intends the Eid prayer, then he does the takbīr for the taḥrīmah, then he recites the thanāʾ, then he says the additional takbīrs thrice raising his hands for each one of them, then he does the taʿawwudh, then he says "*bismillāhir-raḥmānir-raḥīm*" silently, then he recites al-Fātiḥah, then a chapter (it is recommended that it is "*Glorify the name of your Lord the most high*"[509]), then he bows. When he stands for the second unit, he begins with "*bismillāhir-raḥmānir-raḥīm*", then al-Fātiḥah, then the chapter (it is recommended that it is "*The Overwhelming Event*"[510]), then he does the additional takbīrs thrice and he raises his hands in them

---

508 Until it becomes white [Maraqi al-Falah, page 307]. A spear (*rumḥ*) is 12 handspans and as a measure in astronomy according to astronomers and manuscripts, 4.5° altitude, although slight variations (notably 5°) have also been mentioned. However, this needs more research as the height of the spear is almost 2 metres in length. According to my own observations, it is closer to 8°.
509 Chapter 87.
510 Chapter 88.

just as in the first one[511]. This is preferred rather than giving precedence to the additional takbīrs in the second unit over the recitation. If he does give precedence to the additional takbīrs over the recitation, it is permitted.

Then the imam delivers two sermons after the prayer, teaching the rules of the charity of al-Fiṭr in them both[512].

Whoever misses the prayer with imam does not make it up. It is delayed with an excuse to the next day only.

The rules of *al-Aḍḥā*[513] are the same as al-Fiṭr. However, in al-Aḍḥā, food is delayed until after the prayer, he says the takbīr in the street aloud, the imam teaches the sacrificial slaughter and the takbīr of *al-tashrīq* in the sermon, and it is delayed up to three days with an excuse.

The *taʿrīf*[514] is nothing[515]. The takbīr of *al-tashrīq* is wājib upon the imam who is resident in a metropolis and whoever follows him, even if they are a traveller, slave, or woman, from after the Fajr prayer of Arafah[516] until the ʿaṣr prayer of Eid once immediately after every farḍ prayer performed in a recommended congregation according to Abu Hanifah (may Allah show mercy to him). They both[517] said that it is wājib immediately after every farḍ prayer upon whoever prays it, even if they are alone, a traveller, or a villager,

511 The first unit of prayer.

512 The mimbar is not brought out for the two Eid prayers [Al-Asl, Chapter of the Eid Prayer].

513 The Eid taken place on the 10th Dhul-Hijjah.

514 The imitation of people staying at Arafat [Maraqi al-Falah, page 311].

515 Nothing considered, so it is not recommended, rather it is disliked (prohibitively) according to the sound opinion because it is an invention in the religion [Maraqi al-Falah, page 311].

516 The 9th Dhul-Hijjah.

517 Imam Abu Yusuf and Imam Muhammad.

........................................................................................................

........................................................................................................

........................................................................................................

........................................................................................................

........................................................................................................

........................................................................................................

........................................................................................................

........................................................................................................

up until the ʿaṣr prayer of the fifth day after the day of Arafah. The practice is with this and the fatwa is given on it.

There is no harm in the takbīr after the prayer of the two Eids. The takbīr is that he says, "*Allāhu akbar, Allāhu akbar, lā ilāha ill-allāh, Allāhu akbar, Allāhu akbar, wa lillāhil-ḥamd.*[518]"

518 Allah is the greatest x2, there is no god except Allah, Allah is the greatest x2, all praise belongs to Allah.

................................................................................................................................

................................................................................................................................

................................................................................................................................

................................................................................................................................

................................................................................................................................

................................................................................................................................

................................................................................................................................

................................................................................................................................

## Section of the Solar[519] and Lunar Eclipse and Fearful States Prayer

Two units of prayer like the form of the voluntary prayer are sunnah for a solar eclipse with the imam of the Friday prayer or the one given the command from the Head of State but without an adhan, iqāmah, loud recitation, or sermon. Rather, "*Come to the congregational prayer!*" is called out.

Lengthening them, their bowing, and their prostration is sunnah. Then the imam supplicates seated, facing the qiblah if he wishes or standing, facing the people which is better. They say, "*āmīn*" to his supplication until the clearing of the sun is complete. If the imam does not turn up, they pray individually just like the lunar eclipse, intense darkness during the daytime, strong winds, and a fearful state.

---

519 There were two major solar eclipses that occurred in the Medinan period. One total eclipse on the 21st April 627CE corresponding to the 29th Dhul-Qa'dah 5AH from 10:32 to 11:22am and another annular eclipse on the 27th January 632CE corresponding to the 29th Shawwal 10AH from 07:15 to 09:54. See: http://eclipse.gsfc.nasa.gov

## Section of Asking for Rain

It has a prayer without a congregation and it has *istighfār* (seeking forgiveness). Going out for three days walking in worn and used or patched clothing in abasement, humility, fear of Allah ﷻ, lowering their heads, proceeding by giving charity every day before they go out is recommended. Taking animals, elderly people, and babies is recommended. In Mecca and Jerusalem, they gather at the Sacred Mosque and Al-Aqsa Mosque and the people of the City of the Prophet ﷺ should also do it[520].

The imam stands facing the qiblah, raising his hands whilst the people are seated facing the qiblah saying, "*āmīn*" to his supplication. He says quietly or loudly, "*Allāhumma-sqinā ghaythan mughīthan marīʿan murī'an ghadaqan mujallilan saḥḥan ṭabaqan dā'iman*[521]" and whatever resembles it.

There is no flipping of a cloak in it and a non-Muslim subject of a Muslim government does not attend.

---

520 At the prophetic mosque.

521 Oh Allah! Give us an assisting, healthy, productive, abundant, covering, flowing, layering, continuous rain.

........................................................................................................

........................................................................................................

........................................................................................................

........................................................................................................

........................................................................................................

........................................................................................................

........................................................................................................

## Section of the Fear Prayer

It is permitted in the presence of an enemy and with fear of drowning or burning. If people dispute regarding the prayer behind one imam, then he makes them into two groups; one facing the enemy and him with the other praying one unit of a two-unit prayer or two units of a four-unit prayer or the maghrib prayer. This second one proceeds towards the enemy walking and the other comes and the imam prays with them what is remaining and gives salutations alone. Then they go towards the enemy and the first group comes, finishes off without recitation, gives salutations, and then departs. Then they[522] come (if they want) and pray what is remaining with recitation.

If the fear becomes intense, they pray whilst riding, individually, with indications in any direction they are capable of.

It is not valid without the presence of an enemy. Carrying a weapon in the prayer is recommended at the time of fear. If they do not have a dispute regarding the prayer behind one imam, then it is better that each group performs the prayer with an imam just like in a state of security.

522 The other group [Maraqi al-Falah, page 319].

## Section of the Rulings of Funerals

Facing the dying person on their right-hand side is sunnah. Lying down is permitted but his head is raised slightly. He is instructed by mentioning the testification near him without insistence and he is not ordered to say it. Instructing him in the grave is legitimate, it has been said, "He is not to be instructed" and it has been said, "He is not ordered to do it nor prohibited from doing it."

It is recommended for the relatives and neighbours of the dying person to drop in to see him. They should recite the chapter Ya-Sin[523] near him[524]. Some of the later scholars deemed the chapter Raᶜd[525] as good. They differed regarding the removal of a menstruating woman or woman in postpartum bleeding from his presence.

If he dies, his jaws are tightened and his eyes are closed. The one closing his eyes says, *"Bismillāh, wa ᶜalā millati rasūlillāh. Allāhumma yassir ᶜalayhi amrah, wa sahhil ᶜalayhi mā baᶜdah, wa asᶜidhu bliqā'ik, wa-jᶜal mā kharaja ilayhi khayran mimmā kharaja ᶜanhu.*[526]" A piece of iron is placed on his stomach in order that it does not inflate. His hands are placed by his sides and it is not permitted to place them on his chest[527].

---

523 Chapter 36 of the Quran.

524 Based on the hadith, "Recite Ya-Sin over your dying." [Abu Dawud, 3121] and [Ibn Hibban, 345]. Imam Ibn Taymiyyah (d. 728AH) said, "Reciting Ya-Sin over the dying person is recommended." [Al-Ikhtiyarat, pg.91].

525 Chapter 13 of the Quran.

526 In the name of Allah and upon the religion of the Messenger of Allah. Oh Allah make his affair easy for him, make what is after it easy, make him happy with meeting You, and make what he has left towards better than what he has left from.

527 Because it is a practice of the People of the Book [Maraqi al-Falah, page 324].

It is disliked to recite the Quran in his presence until he is washed[528]. There is no harm in informing people of his death. His funeral preparations are hastened.

He is placed on a bed fragranced an odd number of times with incense as soon as he dies and he is placed however is agreeable according to the soundest opinion. His nakedness is covered, then he is stripped of his clothing and given wudu according to the sound opinion (unless he is a minor that does not comprehend the prayer) without rinsing the mouth or nose unless he is in a state of major legal impurity[529]. Water boiled with ground lote-tree leaves and potash is poured on him and if not, then with *qarāḥ* which is pure water. His head and beard are washed with marsh-mallow[530]. He is placed on his left side and washed until the water reaches what[531] is next to the table from him then on his right likewise. He is then sat up resting on him[532] and his stomach is gently wiped. Whatever exits is washed and the washing (*ghusl*) is not repeated. He is then dried-off with a cloth. A perfume mixture is applied to his head and beard, and camphor on his places of prostration[533]. There is no usage of cotton in the washing according to the apparent narrations. His nails and hair are not trimmed nor are his hair or beard combed.

---

528 If the place is prepared for impurity like a toilet or slaughterhouse is, then it is disliked unrestrictedly. If not, and there is no impurity present or someone with their nakedness exposed, then it is not disliked unrestrictedly [Radd al-Muhtar, Chapter of the Rulings of Funerals].

529 It was mentioned by Al-Hulwani, however, it is contrary to what is in the primary legal texts and some found it strange. [Radd al-Muhtar, Chapter of the Rulings of Funerals].

530 *Althaea officinalis.*

531 The side that is [Maraqi al-Falah, page 326].

532 So that he does not fall [Maraqi al-Falah, page 327].

533 They are: The forehead, his nose, both of his hands, both of his knees, and both of his feet [Maraqi al-Falah, page 327].

............................................................................................................

............................................................................................................

............................................................................................................

............................................................................................................

............................................................................................................

A woman washes her husband but not the opposite[534] just like the *Umm al-Walad*[535] does not wash her master. If a woman dies amongst men, they perform tayammum for her using a piece of cloth just like the opposite. If an unmarriageable relative is available, then the deceased is given tayammum without using a piece of cloth. Similarly, the problematic hermaphrodite[536] is given tayammum according to *Ẓāhir al-Riwāyah*. It is permitted for a man and a woman to wash a male or female child that have not reached the age of sexual desirability. There is no harm in kissing the deceased[537].

The man is responsible for the funeral preparations[538] of his wife even if he is financially constrained according to the soundest opinion. The funeral shroud of the one who has no wealth is obligatory upon whoever's maintenance is binding upon him. If no one whose maintenance is obligatory upon him is available then it is from the public treasury. If it is not given due to inability or oppression, then it is obligatory upon the people[539]. The one who is unable to pay for funeral preparations asks someone else.

The shroud of a man is:

1. Sunnah; a full-length shirt[540], a waist-sheet[541], and a wrap[542] from what he used to wear during his life.

---

534 If there is no woman available to wash her, then he performs tayammum for her [Maraqi al-Falah, page 328].

535 The slave-girl who has given birth to her master's child.

536 Someone whose gender cannot be distinguished due to the presence of both male and female genitals.

537 Out of love or seeking blessings [Maraqi al-Falah, page 328]. It was narrated that Abu Bakr kissed the Prophet ﷺ when he died [Al-Bukhari, 1183] also, the Prophet ﷺ kissed Uthman bin Maz'un when he died [Abu Dawud, 3163].

538 Her shrouding and burial [Maraqi al-Falah, page 329].

539 That are able [Maraqi al-Falah, page 329].

540 From the neck to the feet, without a gore and two sleeves [Maraqi al-Falah, page 329].

541 From head to toe [Maraqi al-Falah, page 329].

542 Slightly more than from head to toe [Maraqi al-Falah, page 329].

2. Sufficient; a waist-sheet and a wrap.

White from cotton is preferred. Each of the waist-sheet and the wrap is from head to toe[543]. A sleeve is not made for his full-length shirt, nor a gore[544] or a pocket and its edges are not hemmed. A turban is disliked according to the soundest opinion. It[545] is wrapped from his left then his right. It is tied if feared it will become loose.

For the sunnah, a woman is increased with a headscarf for her face[546] and a piece of cloth for tying her breasts and for the sufficient, a headscarf. Her hair is made into two plaits on her chest above the full-length shirt, then the headscarf over it under the wrap, then the piece of cloth over it.

The shrouds are fragranced with incense an odd number of times before he is wrapped in them. The shroud of necessity is whatever is available.

---

543 With a little extra for tying [Maraqi al-Falah, page 330].

544 A patch for widening the bottom of a shirt to make it easier to walk in.

545 The waist-sheet [Maraqi al-Falah, page 330].

546 And head [Maraqi al-Falah, page 330].

### Section on the Prayer Upon the Deceased

The prayer upon him is a communal farḍ. Its pillars are the takbīrs and standing. Its conditions are six:

1. Islam of the deceased,
2. his purification,
3. his preceding[547], and
4. his presence, the presence of the majority of his body, or half of it with his head.
5. The person praying upon it not be riding without an excuse.
6. The deceased being on the ground. If he is on a riding-beast or in people's arms, the prayer is not permitted according to the chosen opinion unless due to an excuse.

Its sunnahs are four:

1. The standing of the imam adjacent to the deceased whether male or female.
2. The thanā' after the first takbīr.
3. Sending blessings on the Prophet ﷺ after the second one.
4. Supplication for the deceased after the third one. Nothing has

547 The imam of the people [Maraqi al-Falah, page 332].

been specified for this but if he supplicates with what has been transmitted, then it is better and more effectual. From it is what *ʿAwf*[548] memorised from the supplication of the Prophet ﷺ:

*Allāhumma-gh-fir lahu war-ḥamh, wa ʿāfihi waʿfu ʿanh, wa akrim nuzulah, wa wassiʿ madkhalah, wa-ghsilhu bil-mā'i wath-thalaji wal-barad, wa naqqihi minal-khaṭāyā kamā yunaqqāth-thawbul-abyaḍu minad-danas, wa abdilhu dāran khayran min dārih, wa ahlan khayran min ahlih, wa zawjan khayran min zawjih, wa adkhilhul-jannah, wa aʿidhhu min ʿadhābil-qabri wa ʿadhābin-nār*[549].

He gives salutations after the fourth without any supplication according to *Ẓāhir al-Riwāyah.*

He does not raise his hands in other than the first takbīr. If the imam does takbīr a fifth time, he is not followed but his salutations are waited for according to the chosen opinion. An insane person or a child are not sought forgiveness for, rather he says:

*Allāhummaj-ʿalhu lanā faraṭā, waj-ʿalhu lanā ajran wa dhukhran, waj-ʿalhu lanā shāfiʿan wa mushaffaʿā*[550].[551]

---

548 Bin Malik (may Allah be pleased with him). [Sahih Muslim, 963].

549 Oh Allah! Forgive him and show mercy to him, grant him well-being and pardon him, give him a generous serving, widen his place of entering, wash him with water, snow, and hail, cleanse him from sins just as a white garment is cleansed from filth, exchange him a house that is better than his house, a family that is better than his family, and a wife that is better than his wife, enter him into Heaven, and save him from the punishment of the grave and the punishment of Hell. However, the supplication may be said in a language other than Arabic.

550 Oh Allah! Make him a preceded reward for us, make him a reward and a treasure for us, and make him an intercessor for us whose intercession is accepted.

551 Most books mention that people should remain silent after the funeral prayer until the deceased is buried and none of them have mentioned that supplication can or should be done after the funeral prayer:

A man does not stand to make supplication after the funeral prayer because he

## Section on Clarifying the one who has Most Right to the Prayer Over the Deceased and What is Related to it

The head of state has the most right to the prayer of the deceased, then his deputy, then the judge, then the local imam, then the guardian. Whoever has the right of preceding can give permission to someone else. If someone else prays, he repeats it if he wishes. The one who prayed with someone else does not repeat it with him. Whoever has the authority to precede for it has more right than someone that the deceased bequeathed to perform the prayer over him according to the fatwa-given opinion.

If he is buried without a prayer, his grave is prayed over even if he was not washed as long as has not decayed.

If a number of funerals come together, then singling them out for prayer is more appropriate, the most virtuous is given precedence and then the next most virtuous. If they come together and he prays over them once, he makes them into one long row to what is near the qiblah so that the chest of each one is in front of the imam. He pays attention to the order, thus placing the men to what is near the imam, then the children after them, then the hermaphrodites, then the women. However, if they are buried in one grave, they are placed in the opposite of this.

---

already made supplication once because the majority of the funeral prayer is supplication. [Al-Muhit al-Burhani, Chapter of Funerals]

The one who follows the funeral should remain silent and raising one's voice with dhikr, recitation of the Quran, and other than these two is disliked at the funeral. The dislike is a dislike of prohibition in contemporary fatwas and with Majd al-A'immah al-Turkmani. Ala al-Din al-Nasiri said it is leaving what is more preferred. In al-Zahiriyyah: "If he wants to make dhikr of Allah then he does it internally." [Al-Bahr al-Ra'iq, Chapter of Funerals].

..............................................................................................................

..............................................................................................................

..............................................................................................................

..............................................................................................................

..............................................................................................................

The one who finds the imam between two takbīrs does not follow him, rather he waits for the takbīr of the imam and enters with him and conforms with him in his supplication then he makes up what he missed before the lifting of the bier containing the corpse of the deceased. The one who was present for the taḥrīmah of the imam does not wait for the takbīr of the imam. Whoever attends after the fourth takbīr before the salutations has missed the prayer according to the sound opinion. The prayer over him[552] is disliked in a congregational mosque whilst he is in it or outside of it and some people are in the mosque according to the chosen opinion.

Whoever shows signs of life at birth is named, washed, and prayed over. If he shows no signs of life, he is washed[553], according to the chosen opinion, wrapped in a cloth, buried, and not prayed over just like a child that is taken captive with one of his parents, unless one of them or he accepts Islam or neither of them are captured with him.

If a disbeliever has a Muslim relative, he washes him like the washing of an impure cloth, shrouds him in a piece of cloth, and throws him in a hole or he passes him over to the people of his religion.

A rebel[554] or a highway robber killed during hostility, someone who kills by assassination via strangulation, a terrorist with a weapon in the city at night, and someone who is killed due to partisanship, are not prayed over even though they are washed[555]. The one who kills himself is washed and prayed over[556] but not the one who kills one of his parents intentionally.

---

552 The deceased person.
553 Even if his form is not complete [Maraqi al-Falah, page 338].
554 By agreement, even if he is a Muslim [Maraqi al-Falah, page 340].
555 To belittle them and to act as a deterrent to others [Maraqi al-Falah, page 340].
556 Abu Yusuf said, "He is not prayed over." The judge and imam, Ali al-Sughdi used to say, "The soundest opinion with me is that he is not prayed over." [Maraqi al-Falah, page 340].

..........................................................................................

..........................................................................................

..........................................................................................

..........................................................................................

..........................................................................................

..........................................................................................

## Section on Carrying the Bier Containing the Deceased and Burying it

It is sunnah for four men to carry it. They should carry it forty paces[557]. He begins with its front-right on his right[558] (its right is what is in the direction of the left of the carrier), then its rear-right on it[559], then its front-left on his left, then he finishes with the left on it.

Hastening with it is recommended without a gait which is what leads to the disturbance of the deceased. Walking behind it is superior than walking in front of it like the superiority of the obligatory prayer over the voluntary. Raising the voice with remembrance (*dhikr*)[560] and sitting before it is placed down is disliked.

The grave is dug half the height of a man or to the chest. However, if it is increased, it is good. A ledge is made, not a hole unless it is in soft ground[561]. The deceased is made to enter from the direction of the qiblah and the one placing him says, "*Bismillāh, wa ᶜalā millati rasūlillāh.*" He is made to face the qiblah whilst lying on his right-hand side and the knot is undone. Unbaked bricks and reeds are levelled over it[562]. Baked bricks and wood are disliked. Her grave is covered, not his grave[563]. The soil is poured in and the grave is made

557 An extremely weak hadith has been narrated indicating a reward for forty paces, so no attention should be paid to it. See: [Tarikh Ibn Asakir, 27/81].

558 His right shoulder [Maraqi al-Falah, page 341].

559 On his right shoulder [Maraqi al-Falah, page 341].

560 Or the Quran, silence is obligatory upon them [Maraqi al-Falah, page 342].

561 Thus, there is no harm in it nor with using a coffin, even if it is from iron [Maraqi al-Falah, page 343].

562 On the ledge in order to protect his face from the soil [Maraqi al-Falah, page 344].

563 i.e. The grave of a woman is covered until she is buried and she is placed in it.

into a hump not a box. Building over it for decorative purposes is prohibited and it is disliked for solidification after the burial[564]. The is no harm in writing on it in order that the trace does not disappear and it is not belittled[565]. Being buried in houses is disliked due to it been restricted to the prophets (blessings and peace be upon them). Being buried in a tomb is disliked.

There is no harm in burying more than one[566] due to a necessity and a barrier is made between every two people using soil.

Whoever dies in a boat with land far away and harm is feared is washed, shrouded, and thrown into the sea.

The burial is recommended in the locality that he died or was killed in. If he is transported the amount of a mile or two before burial, there is no harm in it but transporting him more than this is disliked. Transporting him after burial is not permitted by consensus unless the land was usurped or taken by right of pre-emption (*shufʿah*)[567]. If he is buried in a grave that was dug for someone else, he is liable for the value of the hole and he is not removed from it. It[568] is exhumed for an item that fell in it, a usurped shroud, or some wealth that is with the deceased. It is not exhumed due to him being placed in other than the direction of the qiblah or on his left.[569]

564 Because it is for permanence and a grave is for annihilation [Maraqi al-Falah, page 344].

565 It has been narrated from Abu Yusuf that it is disliked to write on it [Maraqi al-Falah, page 345].

566 In one grave [Maraqi al-Falah, page 345].

567 The right of obtaining possession of a piece of land or a house for what it cost the former purchaser due to partnership or immediate neighbourship.

568 The grave [Maraqi al-Falah, page 347].

569 Many of our later imams (may Allah have mercy on them) said, "It is disliked to gather with the relative of the deceased so that those who give condolences can come to him, rather, when people return after the burial, let them split up and busy themselves with their affairs and the relative of the deceased with his affair. Sitting

## Section on Visiting Graves

Visiting them is recommended for men and women according to the soundest opinion[570]. Reciting Ya-Sin is recommended due to what was mentioned that

---

at the door of the house for a calamity is disliked because it is the practice of the pre-Islamic people and the Prophet ﷺ prohibited it and it is disliked in the mosque. Hosting from the people of the deceased is disliked because it was legislated for happy times not bad times and it is a reprehensible innovation. He said ﷺ, 'There is no hamstringing in Islam.' (Abu Dawud 3222 and Ahmad 13032) It is the one that used to hamstring a cow or sheep at the grave. It is recommended for the neighbours of the deceased and distant relatives to prepare food for the family of the deceased enough to satiate them for their day and night due to his saying ﷺ, "Make food for the family of Ja'far because that which busies them has occurred" (Abu Dawud 3132 and Al-Tirmidhi 998) and they should insist that they eat because the sorrow will prevent them and weaken them." [Maraqi al-Falah, page 348].

It is disliked to be hosted (with food) by the family of the deceased because it (hosting with food) was legislated in times of happiness not the opposite. It is an abhorrent innovation. It is recommended for the relatives and neighbours to prepare food for them that will satiate them for their day and night [Fath Bab al-Inayah, Chapter of Funerals] and [Maraqi al-Falah, page 347].

Preparing food on the first, third, and seventh day, taking food to the grave at seasonal times, making an invitation to recite the Quran and gather righteous people and reciters for completing the Quran (*khatm*) or reciting the Chapter Al-An'am or Al-Ikhlas is disliked. The upshot is that preparing food when reciting the Quran for the sake of eating is disliked, if it is prepared for the poor, then it is good [Radd al-Muhtar, Chapter of Funerals, 1/603].

570 Imam Birgavi (died 981AH) says in his book *Ziyarat al-Qubur*, "Prayer, circumambulation, kissing, wiping, or asking for help at graves is not permitted by

........................................................................................................................

........................................................................................................................

........................................................................................................................

........................................................................................................................

........................................................................................................................

........................................................................................................................

........................................................................................................................

whoever enters a graveyard and recites Ya-Sin, Allah grants alleviation for them on that day and they receive good deeds according to the number[571] that are in it[572]. It is not disliked to sit at the grave for recitation according to the chosen opinion. However, sitting for other than recitation, standing on them, sleeping, and relieving oneself on them is disliked[573] as well as plucking the grass and plants from the graveyard. However, there is no harm in plucking what is dry from both of them.

---

consensus of the Muslims." Imam al-Ghazali (died 505AH) says in his *Ihya*, "The recommended way to visit graves is to stand with his back towards the qiblah and his face facing the deceased and to give salutations. However, he does not kiss, wipe, or touch it because that is from the customs of the Christians."

571 Of deceased.

572 This is not a hadith with any chain of transmission but has been mentioned in the tafsir of Al-Qurtubi. Imam al-Nawawi mentions in his *Adhkar* with a good chain of transmission from the *Sunan* of Imam al-Bayhaqi that Ibn Umar (may Allah be pleased with them) used to recommend the reading of the first and last parts of the Chapter Al-Baqarah over the grave after the burial (Al-Bayhaqi, 7068).

573 Prohibitively.

.........................................................................................................

.........................................................................................................

.........................................................................................................

.........................................................................................................

.........................................................................................................

.........................................................................................................

.........................................................................................................

.........................................................................................................

## Section of the Rulings of the Martyr

He is washed[574] if he is killed in a state of major legal impurity, as a child, or insane person, or she is a woman menstruating or in postpartum bleeding, or he retained remains of life after the ending of the war by eating, drinking, sleeping, medicating, the passing of a prayer time over him whilst he is conscious, he is moved from the battle not due to fear of the treading of horses, he makes a bequest, sells, buys, or speaks with a lot of speech. However, if any of what was mentioned is found before the ending of the war, he is not someone who retained remains of life.

574 With Imam Abu Hanifah [Maraqi al-Falah, page 354].

# The Book of Fasting

It is refraining from causing something to enter the stomach[575], or what has the ruling of the inner[576], intentionally or erroneously and from the sexual desire of the genitals with intention from its people.

The cause of the obligation of Ramadan is witnessing[577] a part of it and every day of it is a cause for its performance. The performance of it and making up of it is farḍ upon the one who four things are combined in him:

1. Islam.
2. Puberty.
3. Sanity.
4. Knowledge of its obligation for the one who becomes Muslim in non-Muslim lands or merely being in Muslim lands.

Recuperation from an illness, menstruation, postpartum bleeding, and residency are conditional for the obligation of its performance.
Three conditions are conditional for the validity of its performance:

1. Intention.

---

575 From the nose, mouth, or a wound into the inner named *Al-Jā'ifah* [Maraqi al-Falah, page 356]. *Al-Jā'ifah* is a wound that reaches the gastrointestinal tract [Hashiyah al-Tahtawi, Chapter of Fasting]. Based on this, the majority of contemporary Hanafi scholars have said that any kind of injections do not break the fast.
576 Which is the brain [Maraqi al-Falah, page 356]. This was based on the assumption that there was a direct passage from the brain to the gastrointestinal tract which was debated by some scholars of the Hanafi School. However, modern medicine has established that this is not the case, added to the fact that someone is unlikely to survive if food, water, or medicine directly enters the brain. See: [Al-Fatawa al-Hindiyyah, Chapter of Fasting] for a summary of the different opinions.
577 i.e. That the person is present and aware during part of it.

........................................................................................................
........................................................................................................
........................................................................................................
........................................................................................................
........................................................................................................
........................................................................................................
........................................................................................................
........................................................................................................

2. The absence of what negates it from menstruation, postpartum bleeding,
3. and of whatever ruins it.

However, the absence of major legal impurity is not conditional.

Its pillar is withholding from relieving the two desires of the stomach and genitals and whatever is annexed to them.

Its legal ruling is the omission of the obligation from responsibility and reward in the Hereafter.

## Section on the Description of Fasting and its Division

Fasting is divided into six categories:

Farḍ, wājib, sunnah, recommended, voluntary, and disliked.

1. As for the farḍ; it is the performance and making up of the fast of Ramadan, the fast of expiations, and a vow according to the stronger view.
2. As for the wājib; it is making up what he ruined from any voluntary fasts.
3. As for the sunnah; it is the fast of ʿ*Āshūrā*ʾ[578] with the ninth.
4. As for the recommended; it is the fast of three[579] from every month and it is recommended that they are the white days which are the thirteenth, fourteenth, and fifteenth; the fast of Monday and Thursday, the fast of six from Shawwal then it was said that connecting them is better and it was said separating them; and every fast that its requesting and promise for it has been established by the sunnah[580] like the fasting of David (peace be upon him), he would fast one day and not fast another, and this is the most superior fasting and beloved of it to Allah ﷻ.

---

578 The 10th Al-Muharram, the first month of the Islamic calendar.
579 Days [Maraqi al-Falah, page 359].
580 The hadith.

........................................................................................................
........................................................................................................
........................................................................................................
........................................................................................................
........................................................................................................
........................................................................................................
........................................................................................................
........................................................................................................

5. As for the voluntary; it is anything besides this from what its dislike has not been established.

6. As for the disliked; it is two categories: Mildly disliked and prohibitively disliked. The first is like the fast of ᶜ*Āshūrā'* in isolation of the ninth. The second is a fast of the two days of Eid and the days of *tashrīq*[581]. It is also disliked to isolate Friday and isolate Saturday, the Nayrouz or Mahrajan[582] unless it concurs with his habit. Continuous fasting is disliked[583] (even for two days) and it is that he does not break his fast after sunset whatsoever until tomorrow's fast is connected with yesterday's[584]. Fasting all year round is disliked.

---

581 The 11th, 12th, and 13th of Dhul-Hijjah.

582 Because it contains veneration of days that we have been prohibited from venn erating [Maraqi al-Falah, page 361]. These are the names of two Zoroastrian festivals held at the times of the spring and autumn equinoxes.

583 Prohibitively due to the prohibition in the hadith. See: [Al-Bukhari, 1866].

584 A silent fast is also disliked which is that he fasts without saying anything

.....................................................................................................

.....................................................................................................

.....................................................................................................

.....................................................................................................

.....................................................................................................

.....................................................................................................

.....................................................................................................

.....................................................................................................

## Section on What Making Intention from the Night and Specifying it in it is not Conditional and That Which it is Conditional

As for that which specifying the intention is not conditional for nor making it from the night, it is: The performance of Ramadan, a vow whose time is specified, and the voluntary. Thus, it is valid with intention from the night[585] until what is before half of the daytime according to the soundest opinion. Half of the daytime is from the onset of dawn until the time of the greater forenoon[586]. It is also valid with an unspecified intention and the intention of

585 Starting from sunset.

586 This is calculated by dividing the time between dawn and sunset into two equal halves. If the intention is made before the first half, then the fast will be valid due to the presence of intention throughout the majority of the fast. Ibn Abidin mentions, "You already know that the legal daytime is from the rising of dawn until sunset. Know that half of the daytime in every region is before its moving of the sun from the zenith (*al-zawāl*) by half of the time period of its dawn (al-Fajr). Thus, whenever what is remaining for the moving of the sun from the zenith is more than this half, it is valid and if not, then no. The intention is valid in Egypt and Syria before the moving of the sun from the zenith by 15° (azimuth) due to the presence of intention in the majority of the daytime because half of the time period of dawn is not more than 13° in Egypt and 14.5° in Syria. So if what is remaining to the moving of the sun from the zenith is more than half of this period, even by half of a degree, the fast is valid as the shaykh of our teachers *Al-Sa'ihani* accurately verified (may Allah have mercy upon him)" [Radd al-Muhtar, Book of Fasting, Section on the Cause of Fasting Ramadan]. *Note:* It is clear that the degrees being discussed here are the degrees of the sun's azimuth. When I calculated the times for Damascus in Syria, it indicated that they were using a degree of -13.5 at the lowest for the time of dawn. This may well prove

the voluntary even if he is a traveller or ill according to the soundest opinion. The performance of Ramadan is valid with the intention of another obligatory fast for the one who is healthy and resident as opposed to the traveller as it will occur on behalf of the obligatory fast that he intended. The weightier opinion was differed upon regarding when the sick person intended another obligatory fast in Ramadan. The vow whose time is specified with the intention of another obligatory fast is not valid, rather, it will occur on behalf of the obligatory fast that he intended in it[587].

As for the second category, which is what specifying the intention and making it from the night is conditional for, it is: Making up Ramadan, making up what he ruined from any voluntary fasts, the fast of expiations with its different types, and an unspecified vow like him saying, "If Allah cures my sick person, then it is obligatory for me to fast for a day" and the cure happened.

---

that the Muslim astronomers who mentioned degrees such as -20, -19, and -18 for dawn were not using the same measurements that we use today for the sun's altitude. Allah knows best.

587 i.e. In the specified time [Maraqi al-Falah, page 363].

........................................................................................................

........................................................................................................

........................................................................................................

........................................................................................................

........................................................................................................

........................................................................................................

........................................................................................................

........................................................................................................

## Section on What the New Moon is Established by, Fasting the Day of Doubt and Other Than it

Ramadan is established by the sighting of its new moon or by counting *Shaᶜbān*[588] as thirty if the new moon is obscured.

The day of doubt is what follows the twenty-ninth of Shaᶜbān and the side of knowledge and ignorance has levelled on it by the fact that the new moon is obscured. Every fast is disliked on it apart from the voluntary fast that he asserts decisively without ambivalence between it and another fast. If it turns out that it is Ramadan, what he fasted will suffice for it. If he is ambivalent on it[589] between fasting and not fasting, then he will not be someone fasting.

Fasting a day or two at the end of Shaᶜbān is disliked[590]. Anything more than this is not disliked.

The mufti orders the general public to wait on the day of doubt and then to not fast if the time of intention goes and the state is not clear. However, the mufti and the judge fast on it and whoever is from the elite which is whoever is firmly able to control himself from ambivalence in the intention and consideration that it is on behalf the farḍ.

Whoever sees the new moon of Ramadan or Eid al-Fitr alone and his statement is rejected, fasting is binding for him. However, it is not permitted for

---

588 The eighth month of the Islamic calendar.

589 The day of doubt [Maraqi al-Falah, page 366].

590 Preceding with the intent that it is from Ramadan [Maraqi al-Falah, page 366].

........................................................................................................

........................................................................................................

........................................................................................................

........................................................................................................

........................................................................................................

........................................................................................................

........................................................................................................

........................................................................................................

him not to fast due to him being certain of the new moon of *Shawwāl*[591]. If he does not fast in both times[592], he makes it up and no expiation is obligatory for him, even if he broke the fast before the judge rejected him according to the sound opinion.

If there is a defect in the sky due to clouds, dust etc., the statement of one upright[593] or concealed[594] person is accepted for Ramadan according to the sound opinion, even if he testifies on behalf of the testimony of one like him and even if it is a woman, slave, or someone punished for slander who repented. The wording of testifying is not conditional nor is lawsuit[595].

---

591 The tenth month of the Islamic calendar.

592 Ramadan and Shawwāl [Maraqi al-Falah, page 366].

593 He is the one that is good deeds are more than his bad deeds [Maraqi al-Falah, page 368].

594 He is the one whose state is hidden, no sin or uprightness is apparent for him, his statement is accepted [Maraqi al-Falah, page 368].

595 The use of calculations for establishing the new moon was differed upon by the Hanafi scholars. Al-Shurunbulali mentions, "When the statement of mathematicians was differed upon, Ibn Wahban versified: *The statement of the masters of timekeeping is not binding, it was said 'Yes' and some said 'If they are many'*" [Maraqi al-Falah, page 368]. Muhammad bin Salamah from the students of the students of Abu Hanifah held the opinion that if a group of mathematicians held the same opinion then it would be binding. Imam Badr al-Din al-Ayni mentioned, "It was mentioned in Al-Qunyah, 'There is no harm in relying upon the statement of the astronomers.' It was transmitted from Ibn Muqatil, 'There is no harm in relying upon their statement and asking them if a group of them have agreed upon it'... If people were tasked to rely upon astronomical calculation it would be constricted for them because only individuals have knowledge of it and the Legislator only commanded people with what the general populaces of them know. Al-Qushayri said, 'If calculations indicate that the new moon has appeared from the horizon in a manner that if there was no barrier, like cloudiness for example, it would be seen, then this necessitates obligation due to the presence of the legal cause and the literality of seeing is not conditional in relation to obligation because there is agreement that if the one who is imprisoned in

........................................................................................................

........................................................................................................

........................................................................................................

........................................................................................................

........................................................................................................

........................................................................................................

If there is a defect in the sky, the wording of testimony from two free males or one free male and two free females without a lawsuit is conditional for the new moon of Eid al-Fitr.

---

an underground cell knows the completion of the number or by deductive reasoning that the day is from Ramadan, fasting is obligatory upon him even if he did not see the new moon or nobody who saw it informed him'" [Umdah al-Qari, Chapter of is it Said 'Ramadan' or the 'Month of Ramadan'?, Hadith 9981, 10/424].

Were these opinions only in the case of the new moon being obscure? Do they apply to using calculations to reject erroneous sightings only? Are calculations at the level of certainty in our times? The unrestricted statement of these imams seems to indicate not, and Allah knows best. For the beginning of the new lunar month, the Hanafi School requires certainty or strong belief in the presence of the new moon (as will be apparent shortly that even if one or two people saw the new moon and the sky is clear it is still not sufficient according to Abu Hanifah and his companions). The opinion for using calculations was rejected by other scholars in the Hanafi School for four reasons:

1. They were considered doubtful.
2. They necessitated undue hardship for the layman to work out.
3. There are plenty of people who observe moonsighting.

4. Some of them have equated it to the prohibition of seeing a clairvoyant! However, it can be argued that in our times calculations have reached a level close to certainty, the knowledge is readily available to everyone, people have become lax and almost abandoned moonsighting entirely, and the hadith of the clairvoyant does not include the astronomer. The most important matter is the one of authority. If an authority or Muslim ruler declares the start of Ramadan in their respective countries, then it will be binding upon all of the citizens (layman or scholar) to begin fasting. Therefore, the only solution for Muslims in non-Muslim lands is to unite and agree upon a single authority to make the decision. Also, extreme caution should be applied in rejecting positive sightings outside of the modern-day visibility curve maps that have been created because they have not (despite their usefulness) reached the level of absolute certainty and many positive sightings have been affirmed in areas closely outside the visibility curves.

........................................................................................................................

........................................................................................................................

........................................................................................................................

........................................................................................................................

........................................................................................................................

........................................................................................................................

If there is no defect in the sky, then there must be a massive group for Ramadan and Eid al-Fitr[596]. The amount of the massive group is delegated to the opinion of the head of state according to the soundest opinion[597].

If the number is complete based on the testimony of a sole person and the new moon of Eid has not been seen with the sky clear, then it not permitted not to fast. The weightier opinion was differed upon regarding if it was based on the testimony of two upright people. There is no difference of opinion in the permissibility of not fasting if there is a defect in the sky even if Ramadan was established based on the testimony of a sole person.

The new moon of Eid al-Adha is like Eid al-Fitr. The testimony of two upright men or a free man and two free women that have not been punished for slander is conditional for the rest of the new moons. If it is established at the place of ascent of one region, it is binding on everyone else[598] according to the apparent position of the school and fatwa is given on it[599].

596 There is no difference between people in a metropolis and those who come from outside of the metropolis in Ẓāhir al-Riwāyah [Maraqi al-Falah, page 369].

597 It was said, "The people of an area." It was narrated from Abu Yusuf, "Fifty, like *al-Qasāmah* (A unique oath for solving murder cases)." It was narrated from Khalaf, "Five hundred is a small amount in Balkh." Al-Baqqali said, "One thousand is a small amount in Bukhara." Al-Kamal said, "The truth is what has been narrated from Muhammad and Abu Yusuf that consideration is with mass transmission of the report and it coming from every direction." [Maraqi al-Falah, page 369]. These opinions from the early Hanafi scholars seem to refute the idea that the beginning of the new lunar month is literally based on merely seeing the new moon without certainty of its presence.

598 In the east and the west [Rasa'il Ibn Abidin, Tanbih al-Ghafil wa al-Wasnan ala Ahkam Hilal Ramadan].

599 According to the majority of the scholars [Maraqi al-Falah, page 370]. There were a number of earlier Hanafi scholars who advocated regional sighting only,

There is no consideration with the seeing of the new moon during the daytime whether it is before the movement of the sun from the zenith or after it and it will be the following night according to the chosen opinion.

---

however, the position of what is termed as "global sighting" has been transmitted in *Nawādir al-Riwāyah* from Abu Hanifah and should not be abandoned. See [Al-Muhit al-Burhani] and [Al-Fatawa al-Hindiyyah] for more details.

........................................................................................................

........................................................................................................

........................................................................................................

........................................................................................................

........................................................................................................

........................................................................................................

........................................................................................................

........................................................................................................

## Section of Clarifying What Does Not Break the Fast

It is twenty-four things:

1. If he forgetfully eats,
2. drinks,
3. or has sexual intercourse. If the person who forgets has the ability to fast, the one who sees him eating reminds him of it and it is disliked not to remind him. If he does not have strength, then it is better not to remind him.
4. He ejaculates by looking or
5. by pondering, even if he continuously looked or pondered[600].
6. He applies oil.
7. He uses kohl, even if he finds the taste of it in his throat[601].
8. He has cupping performed to him.
9. He backbites.
10. He intends to break the fast but does not break it.
11. Smoke enters his throat not from his own doing or
12. dust, even the dust of flour or
13. a fly or

---

600 Until he ejaculated [Maraqi al-Falah, page 371].
601 Or the colour of it in his saliva [Maraqi al-Falah, page 371].

............................................................................................................

............................................................................................................

............................................................................................................

............................................................................................................

............................................................................................................

............................................................................................................

14. the trace of the taste of medicines in it[602] and he is mindful of his fast.

15. He enters the morning in a state of major legal impurity, even if he continued for an entire day with major legal impurity.

16. He pours water into his urethra or

17. oil.

18. He wades into a river and water enters his ear.

19. He scraped his ear with a stick and dirt came out on it then he entered it repeatedly into his ear.

20. Nasal mucus entered his nose which he snuffed intentionally and swallowed. Phlegm should be spat out in order that his fast is not ruined according to the opinion of Imam Al-Shafi'i.

21. He is overcome by vomit and it returned not from his own doing, even if it fills his mouth according to the sound opinion.

22. He makes himself vomit less than his mouthful according to the sound opinion, even if he causes it to return according to the sound opinion.

23. He eats what is between his teeth and it is less than a chickpea.

24. He chews something like[603] a sesame seed from outside of his mouth until it disintegrates and he does not find the taste of it in his throat[604].

---

602 His throat [Maraqi al-Falah, page 372].
603 The size of it [Maraqi al-Falah, page 374].
604 However, if he swallows it without chewing, the fast is ruined [Hashiyah al-Tahtawi, Chapter of Clarifying What Does Not Break the Fast].

## Section of What Fasting is Ruined by and Expiation with Making it up is Obligatory for it

It is twenty-two things if the fasting person does anything of them willingly, intentionally, and not under compulsion, making it up and expiation is binding upon him. They are:

1. Sexual intercourse in one of the two passages for the doer and the one it is done to.
2. Eating and
3. drinking whether it is what nutrition is taken from or is used for medicine.
4. Swallowing rainwater that enters his mouth.
5. Eating raw meat (even if it is from carrion meat) unless it is maggoted.
6. Eating fat in the opinion of 'The Jurist' Abul-Layth and
7. dried meat by agreement.
8. Eating wheatgrain and
9. nibbling it unless he chews one wheatgrain and it dissipates.
10. Swallowing a grain of wheat,
11. a sesame seed, or similar to it from outside his mouth according to the chosen opinion.

........................................................................................................................

........................................................................................................................

........................................................................................................................

........................................................................................................................

........................................................................................................................

........................................................................................................................

........................................................................................................................

........................................................................................................................

12. Eating Armenian bole[605], unrestrictedly and
13. clay, other than Armenian bole like dry soft clay, if he is accustomed to eating it.
14. A small amount of salt according to the chosen opinion.
15. Swallowing his wife's saliva or
16. his friend's[606], no one other than these two.
17. His eating intentionally after backbiting,
18. after cupping,
19. after touching,
20. after kissing with sexual desire,
21. after lying in bed with a woman without ejaculation,
22. or after oiling his moustache believing that he has broken his fast because of it unless a jurist gave him a fatwa or he heard the hadith and did not know its interpretation according the school. However, if he knew its interpretation, expiation is obligatory upon him.

Expiation is also obligatory upon the woman who complies with a man who is forced[607].

605 This was a type of clay eaten by pregnant women for medicinal purposes, also named "*Rubrica Synopica*." It is red due to the presence of iron oxide.
606 Because he takes delight in it [Maraqi al-Falah, page 377]. Maybe in the case of homosexuals or taking saliva from a pious person.
607 To have sex with her [Maraqi al-Falah, page 378].

........................................................................................................

........................................................................................................

........................................................................................................

........................................................................................................

........................................................................................................

........................................................................................................

........................................................................................................

........................................................................................................

## Section on Expiation and What Omits it From Responsibility

Expiation is omitted by the onset of menstruation, postpartum bleeding, or an illness that permits breaking the fast on its day[608]. It is not omitted from the one who is forced to travel after it becomes binding upon him according to Ẓāhir al-Riwāyah.

Expiation is emancipation of a slave, even if they are not a believer. If he is unable to do so, he fasts two consecutive lunar months not including the day of Eid or the days of tashrīq. If he is unable to fast, he feeds sixty poor people giving them a satiating breakfast and dinner or two breakfasts or two dinners[609] or dinner and a pre-dawn meal. Alternatively, he can give every poor person half a *ṣāʿ*[610] of wheat, its flour, or its porridge, or a full *ṣāʿ* of dry dates or barley, or its value.

One expiation suffices for sexual intercourse and multiple eating on days that performing of expiation did not come in between it, even if from two Ramadans according to the sound opinion. If the performing of expiation came in between, one expiation does not suffice according to Ẓāhir al-Riwāyah.

608 The day of ruining that necessitates the expiation.
609 On two separate days.
610 An archaic measure of volume equivalent to approximately 3 litres or less.

## Section of What Ruins the Fast and Necessitates Making it up Without Expiation

It is fifty-seven things[611]:

1. If the fasting person eats raw rice,
2. dough,
3. flour,
4. a large amount of salt in one go,
5. clay (not Armenian) that he is not accustomed to eating,
6. a date-stone,
7. cotton,
8. paper,
9. quince that has not been cooked,
10. a moist walnut, or
11. he swallows a pebble,
12. iron,
13. dirt,
14. a stone, or

611 Not exhaustively. The most common examples are mentioned.

.............................................................................................................

.............................................................................................................

.............................................................................................................

.............................................................................................................

.............................................................................................................

.............................................................................................................

.............................................................................................................

15. he has an enema,
16. inhales snuff, or
17. is made to swallow by pouring something in his throat, according to the soundest opinion[612], or
18. he places drops of oil into his ear or
19. water, according to the soundest opinion[613], or
20. he medicates a stomach wound, or
21. a head wound with medicine and it reaches his gastrointestinal tract or his brain,
22. rain or
23. snow enter his throat, according to the soundest opinion, and he did not swallow it from his own doing,
24. he breaks his fast erroneously by the preceding of water used for gargling into his gastrointestinal tract, or
25. he breaks his fast under coercion, even with sexual intercourse, or
26. she is coerced into sexual intercourse, or
27. she breaks her fast out of fear for herself becoming too ill to work, whether she is a slave-girl or married, or
28. somebody poured water into his stomach whilst he is sleeping, or

---

612 This is related to having an enema (clyster) and what is mentioned after it [Maraqi al-Falah, page 381].

613 In *Al-Muhit*: 'The sound opinion is that it does not break the fast.' [Maraqi al-Falah, page 381]. The correct opinion is that it does not ruin the fast due to their being no passage to the stomach unless someone has a perforated eardrum.

29. he eats intentionally after his eating forgetfully, even if he knows the narration[614] according to the soundest opinion, or

30. he has sexual intercourse forgetfully, then has sexual intercourse intentionally, or

31. he eats after he made intention during the daytime and did not make his intention during the night,

32. he enters the morning as a traveller, then intended residency, then eats, or

33. travelled after entering the morning as a resident, then eats, or

34. he abstains without the intention to fast or the intention not to fast, or

35. he has the pre-dawn meal, or

36. sexual intercourse doubting the onset of dawn and it had begun, or

37. he breaks his fast with the belief of the sunset and the sun is remaining, or

38. he ejaculates due to sex with a dead woman,

39. an animal,

40. rubbing against the thigh,

41. rubbing against the stomach,

42. kissing, or

43. touching, or

614 "If he forgets, then eats and drinks, let him complete his, because it is only Allah that fed him and gave him drink." [Al-Bukhari, 1933].

44. he ruins a fast that is not the performance of Ramadan, or

45. someone has sex with her whilst she is sleeping[615], or

46. placed drops of water into her vagina, according to the soundest opinion[616], or

47. enters his finger moistened with water or oil into his anus, or

48. she enters it[617] into her inner vagina, according to the chosen opinion, or

49. he enters a piece of cotton into his anus and causes it to disappear or

50. in her inner vagina, or

51. he causes smoke to enter his throat from his own doing, or

52. he forcefully vomits, even if it is less than a mouthful according to Ẓāhir al-Riwāyah. Abu Yusuf (may Allah ﷻ have mercy upon him) stipulated a condition of a mouthful and it is the sound opinion, or

53. he causes what overcame him of vomit to return and it was a mouthful whilst he, is remembering[618], or

54. he eats what is between his teeth and it is the amount of a chickpea, or

---

615 Or after her going insane [Maraqi al-Falah, page 384].

616 The correct opinion concerning the inner vagina is that it does not ruin the fast, due to the absence of a passage to the stomach.

617 Her wet finger.

618 His fast.

55. he intended the fast during the daytime after he ate forgetfully before making his intention in the day, or

56. he became unconscious, even for the entire month, except that he does not make up the day that the unconsciousness occurred in or it occurred during his night or

57. he became insane but it does not last the entire month.

The making up of it is not obligatory for him with his coming to his senses during the night or day after missing the time of the intention, according to the sound opinion[619].

---

619 In Al-Fath (Fath al-Qadir) the making up of it is obligatory for him with his coming to his senses, unreservedly [Maraqi al-Falah, page 385].

........................................................................................................

........................................................................................................

........................................................................................................

........................................................................................................

........................................................................................................

........................................................................................................

........................................................................................................

........................................................................................................

## Section on When it is Necessary to Abstain for the Rest of the Day

Abstinence is obligatory[620] for the rest of the day upon the one whose fast is ruined, a menstruating woman and a woman in postpartum bleeding if they become pure after the onset of dawn, a child that reaches puberty and a disbeliever that becomes Muslim after the onset. Making up is obligatory upon them except the last two.

620 It was said, "Recommended" [Maraqi al-Falah, page 386].

## Section on What is Disliked for the Fasting Person, What is Not Disliked, and What is Recommended

Seven things are disliked for the fasting person:

1. Tasting something.
2. Chewing it without an excuse.
3. Chewing mastic.
4. Kissing and
5. sexual contact if he does not feel safe for himself (in regards to both of them) from ejaculation or sexual intercourse according to Ẓāhir al-Riwāyah.
6. Gathering saliva in the mouth[621] and swallowing it.
7. What he believes will weaken him like phlebotomy and cupping.

There are nine things that are not disliked for the fasting person:

1. Kissing and
2. sexual contact with safety[622].
3. Oiling the moustache.
4. Kohl.

---

621 Intentionally.
622 From ejaculation or sexual intercourse.

.................................................................................................................................

.................................................................................................................................

.................................................................................................................................

.................................................................................................................................

.................................................................................................................................

.................................................................................................................................

.................................................................................................................................

.................................................................................................................................

5. Cupping[623].
6. Phlebotomy.
7. Brushing one's teeth at the end of the day, rather it is sunnah just like the beginning of it, even if it is soft or moistened with water.
8. Rinsing one's mouth and inhaling water into the nostrils for other than wudu and bathing.
9. Wrapping the body with a wet garment for cooling purposes, according to the opinion that fatwa is given on.

Three things are recommended:

1. The pre-dawn meal.
2. Delaying it.
3. Hastening of breaking the fast on a day that is not cloudy.

---

623 That does not weaken him.

..............................................................................................

..............................................................................................

..............................................................................................

..............................................................................................

..............................................................................................

..............................................................................................

..............................................................................................

## Section on Impediments[624]

For whoever fears an increase in illness[625] or a delay in recovery, a pregnant woman, a breastfeeding woman who fears a reduction in intellect, death, or illness for herself or her child whether it is a relative or suckling. The fear that is considered is based on strong belief due to [626]experience or the informing of a medic[627]. Also, for whoever extreme thirst or hunger occurs to and they fear dying from it[628].

Not fasting is permitted for the traveller[629] but him fasting is more preferred if it does not harm him and the majority of his travelling companions are not fasting nor sharing the provisions. If they are sharing or not fasting, then it is better for him not to fast to keep in conformity with the group.

Making a bequest is not obligatory upon the one who dies before the disappearance of his excuse due to illness, travel, and what is analogous to it as has preceded. They make up what they were able to make up according to the amount of residency and health. Consecutiveness is not conditional in making up. If another Ramadan comes it is given precedence over making up and there is no compensation due to delaying it until then.

---

624 That permit breaking the fast or make a person exempt from the fast.
625 Whether in quantity or quality if they were to fast [Maraqi al-Falah, page 390].
626 Prior.
627 Muslim, professional, outwardly upright [Maraqi al-Falah, page 391].
628 Or a reduction in intellect or loss of some the senses and it was not due to him tiring himself out [Maraqi al-Falah, page 391].
629 It should be noted that he must be considered a traveller by leaving his city boundaries before dawn otherwise he must complete the fast on his journey.

........................................................................................................................

........................................................................................................................

........................................................................................................................

........................................................................................................................

........................................................................................................................

........................................................................................................................

........................................................................................................................

Not fasting is permitted for a decrepit old man and woman but the compensation is obligatory for both of them[630]. For every day it is half a *ṣāᶜ* of wheat[631], like the one who made a vow of endless fasting then became too weak to do it; if he is unable to give the compensation due to his poverty, he asks forgiveness from Allah ﷻ and asks Him to cancel it out.

If the expiation of an oath or murder is obligatory upon him and he does not find that which he can perform expiation with of emancipation[632] and he is a decrepit old man or he did not fast[633], then compensation is not permitted for him.

It is permitted for the voluntary performer to break the fast without an excuse according to one narration[634]. Hospitality is an excuse, according to the stronger view, for the guest and the host and he has glad tidings of this majestic benefit[635]. If he breaks his fast, in any case, making up is obligatory for him unless he initiated as a voluntary performer on five days: The two days of the two Eids and the days of tashrīq[636]. Thus, making them up is not obligatory for him due to ruining them according to Ẓāhir al-Riwāyah.

630 Likewise, for the one who has no hope of ever being able to fast again before they die.

631 Or its value.

632 Or feeding and clothing [Maraqi al-Falah, page 393].

633 Until he became a decrepit [Maraqi al-Falah, page 393].

634 From Abu Yusuf [Maraqi al-Falah, page 393].

635 Due to the narration, "Whoever breaks his fast for the right of his brother, the reward of fasting a thousand days are written for him and when he makes up a day, the reward of two-thousand days of fasting are written for him." [Maraqi al-Falah, page 394]. There is no basis to this narration, the earliest mention I found of it was by the author of Al-Jawharah al-Nayyirah (800AH) and the author of Durar al-Hukkam (885AH) despite the author saying it is in some earlier books.

636 See: Section of Eid.

......................................................................................................

......................................................................................................

......................................................................................................

......................................................................................................

......................................................................................................

......................................................................................................

......................................................................................................

## Section of What Necessitates Fulfilment of it From Vows of Fasting, Prayer, and Other Than These Two

If he makes a vow of something, the fulfilment of it is obligatory for him if three conditions are met in it:

1. That there is something that is obligatory[637] from its category.
2. That it is intended[638].
3. That it is not obligatory[639].

Therefore, wudu is not binding due to a vow of it[640] nor a prostration of recital nor visiting the sick nor obligatory acts due to a vow of them.

It is valid with emancipation, spiritual retreat, prayer other than the obligatory prayer, and fasting.

If he makes an unrestricted vow[641] or one attached to a condition[642] and it occurs, the fulfilment of it is obligatory for him.

---

637 Like the prayer, fasting, and charity.

638 In and of itself, not due to other than it like wudu [Maraqi al-Falah, page 396].

639 A fourth condition has been added that the vow cannot be impossible [Maraqi al-Falah, page 396]. It should also be noted that the vow must be verbalised with the correct wording for making a vow.

640 Nor recitation of the Quran [Maraqi al-Falah, page 396].

641 Like him saying, "A two-unit prayer is binding upon me for Allah." [Maraqi al-Falah, page 397].

642 Like him saying, "If Allah grants me a child, then I must feed ten poor people." [Maraqi al-Falah, page 397].

..........................................................................................

..........................................................................................

..........................................................................................

..........................................................................................

..........................................................................................

..........................................................................................

..........................................................................................

The vow to fast on the two Eids and the days of tashrīq is valid, according to the chosen opinion, and not fasting them and making them up is obligatory. If he fasts them, it will suffice him with prohibition.

We have annulled the specifying of time, place, dirham[643], and poor person. Thus, the fast of Rajab will suffice him for his vow to fast Shaʿbān, a two-unit prayer in Egypt will suffice him if he vowed to perform them in Mecca, giving a dirham in charity instead of a dirham that he has already specified for giving in charity, and spending on Zayd that is a poor person with his vow[644] for Amr.

If he attaches the vow to a condition, it will not suffice him for what he does before the appearance of its condition.

643 A silver coin used for purchases weighing approximately 2.975g.
644 To spend on.

## Section of Spiritual Retreat

It is residing with its[645] intention in a mosque[646] where the congregation is physically established in it for the five prayers[647]. Therefore, it is not valid in a mosque where the congregation for prayer[648] is not established according to the chosen opinion.

Spiritual retreat for a woman is in the mosque of her house, it is a place that she has designated for prayer in.

Spiritual retreat is three categories:

1. Obligatory in that which is vowed.
2. A communal[649] emphasised sunnah in the last ten of Ramadan.
3. Recommended for anything else[650].

Fasting is a condition for the validity of the vowed only. Its minimum volun-

645 Spiritual retreat.
646 It is not valid in a place other than a mosque.
647 Abu Yusuf and Muhammad said it is valid in any mosque [Hashiyah al-Tahtawi, Chapter of Spiritual Retreat].
648 All of the five prayers.
649 It is a communal sunnah for every country like the funeral prayer [Al-Insaf fi Hukm al-I'tikaf].
650 i.e. in any time he wishes other than the last ten and it is not vowed [Maraqi al-Falah, page 401].

........................................................................................................

........................................................................................................

........................................................................................................

........................................................................................................

........................................................................................................

........................................................................................................

........................................................................................................

........................................................................................................

tarily is a short time period even if he is walking[651], according to fatwa-given opinion.

He does not leave it[652] unless for a legal need such as the Friday prayer, natural such as urinating, or compelling such as the collapsing of the mosque, being removed by a tyrant forcefully, the breaking up of his family, and fear for himself or his belongings from renegades. So, he enters another mosque immediately. If he leaves without an excuse, the obligatory is ruined[653] and anything else[654] ends with it[655].

The eating of the person in spiritual retreat, his drinking, his sleeping, and his sale contract for what he needs for himself and his family is in the mosque[656]. The bringing of the sale item to it[657] is disliked as well a contract that is for business. Silence is disliked if he believes it to be an act of worship. Sexual intercourse and its incentives are prohibited. It[658] becomes invalid due to his sexual intercourse and due to ejaculation from its[659] incentives.

---

651 i.e. through the mosque.

652 His place of spiritual retreat, so it includes a woman that is performing spiritual retreat in the mosque of her house [Maraqi al-Falah, page 401]. A note should be made that the following rulings of leaving only apply to the vowed spiritual retreat, as for the voluntary, then a person can leave whenever they wish with no consequence.

653 And there is no sin upon him [Maraqi al-Falah, page 402]. Abu Yusuf and Muhammad said that if he leaves for the majority of the day, it is ruined and if not, then no [Maraqi al-Falah, page 402].

654 Such as the voluntary.

655 Leaving.

656 Only.

657 The mosque. However, bringing the item is prohibitively disliked and conducting the contract is mildly disliked.

658 The spiritual retreat.

659 Sexual intercourse.

.............................................................................................................

.............................................................................................................

.............................................................................................................

.............................................................................................................

.............................................................................................................

.............................................................................................................

.............................................................................................................

Nights are also obligatory for him with his vow of spiritual retreat of days[660]. Days are obligatory for him with his vow of consecutive nights even if he did not make consecutiveness a condition according to Ẓāhir al-Riwāyah. Two nights are obligatory for him with his vow of two days. The intention of the daytime specifically, exclusive of nights, is valid. If he makes a vow of spiritual retreat of a month and intends the month specifically or the nights specifically, his intention has no effect unless he explicitly states the exception[661].

Spiritual retreat is legal based on the Quran and the Sunnah. It is from the most honourable of actions if it from sincerity. From its good qualities is that in it is the emptying of the heart from the affairs of the world, submitting of the self to the Master, adhering to His worship in His house, and taking protection by His fortress. Ata'[662] said, "The parable of the person in spiritual retreat is the parable of a man who frequents the door of a great ruler for his need. The person in spiritual retreat says, 'I won't leave until He forgives me.'"

660 Because the mentioning of days with the plural wording means the entering in them of what is adjacent to them from the nights [Maraqi al-Falah, page 403].
661 Because the month is a noun for a specific measure that includes days and nights [Maraqi al-Falah, page 404].
662 Bin Abu Rabah, the successor, the student of Ibn Abbas (may Allah be pleased with them) and one of the teachers of The Great Imam (Abu Hanifah) [Maraqi al-Falah, page 405].

# Conclusion

This is what has been facilitated for the weak and despicable one with the divine care of his Master, the strong and capable. Praise belongs to Allah who guided us to this and we would never had been guided unless Allah guided us. May Allah send blessings upon our lord Muhammad and our master Muhammad, the seal of His prophets, and upon his family, his companions, his progeny, and whoever follows him. We ask Allah ﷻ, seeking a means[663], that He makes it purely for His noble sake, that He benefits by it a benefit that is universal, and that He makes the immense reward copious by it.

This is the end of the translation of "The Light of Clarification and Salvation of the Souls". I added an appendix in the subject area of Zakah for additional benefit.

BILAL BROWN

663 To Him via the chosen merciful Prophet [Maraqi al-Falah, page 407].

# The Book of Zakāh

Zakah[664] is the obligatory[665] transferral of ownership[666] of a portion of one's wealth with intention[667] as stipulated by the sacred law to those who are eligible recipients[668] without reciprocation[669].

The conditions of it being obligatory are:

1. Islam
2. Puberty
3. Intellect
4. Freedom

The cause of it being obligatory is ownership of the threshold (*niṣāb*) at the two ends of the lunar year, free of any debts that are being requested[670] and basic needs[671].

---

664 It is coupled with the obligation to pray eighty-two times in the Quran and was made obligatory in the year 2 AH.

665 This excludes voluntary charity, commonly known as *ṣadaqah*. Scholars differed as to whether it is immediately obligatory or not. Abu Bakr al-Razi said it is not and Al-Karkhi said that it is immediate.

666 This excludes absolving a debt or using the wealth for construction projects.

667 This excludes wealth that is given without intention.

668 This excludes those who are not eligible to receive zakah.

669 This excludes a sale transaction.

670 This excludes expiations, vows, obligatory hajj etc. If the debt is a long term one where the full amount is not being requested immediately then three opinions have been mentioned:

a) The full amount can be deducted.

b) The amount for the year can be deducted.

c) The amount for the month can be deducted. See: *Radd al-Muhtar*, Chapter of Zakah.

671 Such as property used for living in, clothing, furniture, work tools etc.

........................................................................................................................

........................................................................................................................

........................................................................................................................

........................................................................................................................

........................................................................................................................

........................................................................................................................

........................................................................................................................

Whoever gives away all of their wealth in charity, the obligation of zakah is omitted, even if they did not intend it[672].

There is no zakah in lost or uncollectable wealth[673].

Any newly acquired similar wealth throughout the year is added to the original wealth. Falling below the threshold during the lunar year does not prevent the obligation of zakah. However, if a person loses all their wealth or falls into a negative balance, then the lunar year is omitted.

Zakah is omitted by the perishing[674] of the threshold after the lunar year, if part of it perishes, then its percentage is omitted.

Paying the value is permitted. Whoever possesses the threshold and pays zakah in advance before the end of the lunar year or more years, then it is valid.

Zakah is only obligatory on four categories of wealth:

1. Livestock
2. Gold and silver[675]
3. Trade items[676]
4. Crops and fruits

---

672 Analogy dictates that it would not be omitted, this is the opinion of Imam Zufar. However, legal discretion (*istiḥsān*) is applied because the obligatory amount is part of the threshold and the pillar is transferral of ownership in a charitable manner, which has occurred.

673 e.g. Stolen wealth, wealth whose location has been forgotten, or a debt owed that is being rejected etc.

674 As opposed to it being used up or caused to perish.

675 This excludes all other metals and precious gems.

676 This includes fiat money that is in circulation, digital assets, and anything used with the intention of buying and selling.

............................................................................................................

............................................................................................................

............................................................................................................

............................................................................................................

............................................................................................................

............................................................................................................

............................................................................................................

## Zakah of Livestock

The only categories of livestock which are subject to zakah are enumerated below[677]:

| TYPE OF ANIMAL | THRESHOLD |
|---|---|
| camels | 5 |
| Sheep and goats | 40 |
| Cows, bulls, Oxen and buffaloes | 30 |

In order for zakah to be taken from these categories of livestock the following conditions must be satisfied:

1. The animals concerned must attain a threshold (minimum amount required).
2. They have to be in one's ownership for one lunar year.
3. They should have pastured by themselves; that is, grazing most of the year in the available pasture (for at least six months) otherwise it is not classed as livestock in legal terms.
    - Animals which are used for riding or for carrying loads are not subject to zakah.

677 Imam Abu Hanifah held the opinion that zakah is payable on horses to the amount of one dinar (4.25g of gold) per horse. Imam Abu Yusuf and Imam Muhammad said that there is no zakah on horses.

- If all the livestock were to die after zakah being obligatory then zakah is void.
- The value of the livestock due may be paid as zakah, or a combination of both.
- The rate of zakah varies according to the type of the animal as given by the following tables:

.............................................................................................................

.............................................................................................................

.............................................................................................................

.............................................................................................................

.............................................................................................................

.............................................................................................................

.............................................................................................................

## Camels

| NO. OF CAMELS | RATE OF ZAKAH |
|---|---|
| up until 4 | No zakah |
| From 5-9 | 1 goat/sheep |
| 10-14 | 2 goats/sheep |
| 15-19 | 3 goats/sheep |
| 20-24 | 4 goats/sheep |
| 25-35 | 1 two-year-old *female* camel |
| 36-45 | 1 three-year-old *female* camel |
| 46-60 | 1 four-year-old *female* camel |
| 61-75 | 1 five-year-old *female* camel |
| 76-90 | 2 × three-year-old *female* camel |
| 91-120 | 2 × four-year-old *female* camel |
| From here calculation recommences from the beginning, so for every 5 camels above 120, a goat/sheep is added to the rate | |
| 145-149 | 2 × four-year-old + 1 × two-year-old *female* camel |
| 150 | 3 × four-year-old *female* camel |
| From here calculation recommences from the beginning, so for every 5 camels above 150, a goat/sheep is added to the rate. | |
| 175-185 | 3 × four-year-old + 1 × two-year-old *female* camel |
| 186-195 | 3 × four-year-old + 1 × three-year-old *female* camel |
| 196-200 | 4 × four-year-old |
| From here pattern is followed as is after 150 | |

## Goats/Sheep

| NO. OF GOATS/ SHEEP | RATE OF ZAKAH |
| --- | --- |
| up until 39 | No zakah |
| 40-120 | 1 goat/sheep |
| 121-200 | 2 goats/sheep |
| 201-399 | 3 goats/sheep |
| 400 | 4 goats/sheep |
| Thereafter, the rate is 1 goat/sheep for each 100 | |

.......................................................................................................................

.......................................................................................................................

.......................................................................................................................

.......................................................................................................................

.......................................................................................................................

.......................................................................................................................

.......................................................................................................................

## Cows, Bulls, Oxen and Buffaloes

| NO. OF ANIMALS | RATE OF ZAKAH |
|---|---|
| up until 29 | No zakah |
| 30-39 | 1 two-year-old |
| 40 | 1 three-year-old |
| 41-59 | 1 three-year-old plus 2.5% of it for every extra animal. |
| 60-69 | 2 × two-year-old |
| 70–79 | 1 three-year-old and 1 two-year-old |
| 80–89 | 2 × three-year-old |
| Thereafter, the rate is a two-year-old for every 30 and a three-year-old for every 40 | |

## Zakah of Gold and Silver

Whether the gold or silver has been minted, made into jewellery, containers, or not, zakah is obligatory regardless if trade is intended with them or not, if they reach the threshold. Each one is added to the other according to the value.

The threshold of gold is twenty *mithqāls*[678]. Half a mithqāl is payable for twenty[679].

The threshold of silver is two hundred *dirhams*[680]. Five dirhams are payable for every two hundred[681].

---

678 Each mithqāl weighs 4.25g. The total is 85g. The mithqal weight of the classical Islamic gold *dīnār* can be determined with a high degree of precision. In this case we must not proceed from the coins themselves, but rather from the glass weights that have been produced for their gauging. The most exact glass weights from the year 780 CE that have been discovered so far and that agree up to a third of a milligram result in an average weight of 4.231g. See: http://numismatics.org/digitallibrary/ark:/53695/nnan139398 for more information.

679 2.5%. From here, Imam Abu Hanifah says there is no zakah until it reaches twenty-four mithqāls and so on for every four mithqāls, Imam Abu Yusuf and Imam Muhammad said that the percentage of 2.5% is paid regardless.

680 A silver coin weighing 2.975g. The weight of 7 dinars was equivalent to 10 dirhams, see: *Al-Hidayah, Al-Ikhtiyar, Radd al-Muhtar.*

681 Again, 2.5%. From here, Imam Abu Hanifah says there is no zakah until it reaches two hundred and forty dirhams and so on for every forty dirhams, Imam Abu Yusuf and Imam Muhammad said that the percentage of 2.5% is paid regardless.

..........................................................................................

..........................................................................................

..........................................................................................

..........................................................................................

..........................................................................................

..........................................................................................

..........................................................................................

..........................................................................................

Dominance is considered in both of them, so if the gold is less than 12-carat or 500 fineness for silver then there is no zakah[682] and they are considered as ordinary items.

682 Unless the amount of gold in them reaches the weight of the threshold or they are for trade. If the gold or silver is 50%, then there is no zakah due to the basis being non-obligation and doubt occurring in the legal cause.

........................................................................................................................

........................................................................................................................

........................................................................................................................

........................................................................................................................

........................................................................................................................

........................................................................................................................

........................................................................................................................

........................................................................................................................

## Zakah of Trade Items

There is no zakah on items unless they are for trade and their value[683] reaches the threshold of either gold or silver. Their value is added to any gold or silver.

683 Not their sale price. This is calculated according to the day that the zakah is due. It should be noted that in the time of the Messenger of Allah ﷺ and for over a thousand years after it, one gold dīnār (4.25g of gold) was approximately equivalent in value to ten dirhams (29.75g of silver) with little fluctuation. In the past century, the price of silver has been extremely volatile mainly due to supply and demand and at the time of writing stands at approximately 85 (i.e. It would take 85 ounces of silver to buy one ounce of gold). Most Muslim scholars have chosen the view that the gold threshold should be adopted due to its stability and being the true basis of currency, whereas some have chosen the view to adopt the silver threshold, seeing it as more beneficial for the poor.

## Zakah of Crops and Fruit

A tenth is obligatory on whatever is watered naturally or by irrigation, whether large or small[684]. Reeds, firewood, and weeds[685] are excluded unless the land is being specifically used to grow these. Whatever is watered by a waterwheel or by buckets, then one-twentieth is obligatory. There is nothing obligatory for hay and dried leaves.

Land expenses or taxes are not taken into account. There is one tenth on honey, whether large or small, if it is taken from eligible land.

There is nothing obligatory on what is taken from the sea, like pearls, ambergris, and coral. Nor from what is found in mountains, like plaster, limestone, rubies, emeralds etc.

---

684 Imam Abu Yusuf and Imam Muhammad said that it is not obligatory until it reaches five *awsuq*. The *wasq* is container the equivalent of sixty *ṣāʿ*. It is approximately 165 litres, making the threshold 825 litres in total.

685 Likewise, anything that is normally removed from the land and discarded.

## Recipients of Zakah

1. The poor. This is someone who possesses less than the threshold from any type of wealth beyond their basic needs. It is not permitted for this person to ask for zakah.
2. The destitute. This is someone who possesses next to nothing, i.e. they only have enough to get by on a daily basis. It is permitted for this person to ask for zakah.
3. The person working to collect zakah. They can take a wage for what suffices them and their families, even if they are already wealthy.
4. Slaves. This is the slave who has a contract of emancipation with their master. The zakah can be paid to fulfil the contract.
5. The debtor. If their debt takes them under the threshold, zakah can be given to them directly in order to pay off their debt.
6. In the cause of Allah ﷻ. This is the soldier who has been cut off from his troops according to Imam Abu Yusuf and it is the correct opinion. According to Imam Muhammad, it is the person on hajj who has been cut off from his group. It has also been said that the students of sacred knowledge are included in it.[686]
7. The traveller. This is someone who may have wealth in their

686 See: *Al-Lubab fi Sharh al-Kitab* and *Bada'i al-Sana'i*

country but does not have access to it. They can be given enough zakah to enable them to return to their country but no more.

As for the eighth category mentioned in the Quran, this has been abrogated or suspended by silent consensus of the companions.

Zakah is not paid to:

1. A disbeliever. Nor to the people of innovation according to the chosen opinion[687].
2. A rich person. This is someone who possesses the threshold from any type of wealth beyond their basic needs. Nor to the pre-pubescent son or slave of a rich person.
3. Ascendants and descendants. Such as one's parent or grandparent, child or grandchild.
4. One's wife. Nor to the husband with Imam Abu Hanifah, whereas Imam Abu Yusuf and Imam Muhammad permitted the wife to pay it to her husband.
5. His slave or contract-slave.
6. A Hashemite. Nor the freed-slave of a Hashemite. This is one of the descendants of Ali, Abbas, Ja'far, Aqil, and Harith bin Abdul Muttalib. Some said that a Hashemite can pay to another Hashemite according to Imam Abu Hanifah.

Zakah is also not given to building projects, such as the building of a mosque, a bridge, or military barracks[688]. It is not used for the funeral shroud of a dead

687 This is mentioned in *Al-Fatawa al-Bazzaziyyah.*
688 This is because transferral of ownership is not complete without taking possession.

person or to pay of a dead person's debt-however, if it is used to pay off a living poor person's debt with his command, then it is valid[689].

If one poor person is given the amount of the threshold or more, it is valid but disliked[690]. It is permitted to pay it to whoever possesses less than the threshold even if he is healthy and earning a living.

It is disliked to transport it to a different country unless it is to a relative or someone who is needier.

---

689 The one who takes possession will become like an agent on behalf of the poor person.

690 This is if he still has the threshold in his possession after using it for his needs and giving it to his family members.

........................................................................................................

........................................................................................................

........................................................................................................

........................................................................................................

........................................................................................................

........................................................................................................

........................................................................................................

........................................................................................................

## Charity of Eid al-Fitr

It is *wājib* on every free Muslim that possesses the amount of the threshold from any type of wealth beyond his basic needs on behalf of himself, his pre-pubescent children, and his slaves for service (even if they are disbelievers) only.

It is half a *ṣāʿ*[691] of wheat or its flour or a full *ṣāʿ* of barley or its flour, dates, raisins, or the value of any of these.

It is obligatory at the onset of dawn on the day of Eid al-Fitr. If he pays it earlier[692], it is valid. If he delays it, then he must still pay it.

---

691 An archaic measure of volume equivalent to approximately 3 litres or less.

692 Even before Ramadan.

## Zakah of Debts Owed

Zakah is to be paid on debts owed to the person paying zakah. This falls under three categories:

1. A strong debt. This is the exchange of a loan and payment of a trade item if possession has been taken of the item and the buyer affirms the debt. If the buyer is bankrupt or denying the debt, then the burden of proof is upon the debtee. The obligation of zakah is delayed (but not omitted) until possession of part of the payment is taken.

2. A medium debt. This is the exchange of what is not a trade item, like the payment for the sale of work clothing, work tools, and a house for residence[693]. No zakah is due until possession of the threshold is taken. Consideration is taken for what has passed from the zakah year from the time of the payment becoming binding in the liability of the buyer.

3. A weak debt. This is the exchange of what is not wealth, like the dowry, a will, a payment for marital release, settlement for intentional murder, and an indemnity payment[694]. No zakah is obligatory upon it until possession of the threshold is taken and a lunar year passes over it[695].

---

693 Payment owed for services and rentals comes under this category. See: *Al-Mabsut*, Chapter of Zakah.

694 Owed wages to the employee come under this category. See: *Al-Mabsut*, Chapter of Zakah.

695 This is with Imam Abu Hanifah. Imam Muhammad and Imam Abu Yusuf said that zakah is obligatory on all types of debt (even before taking possession of them) according to their percentages once possession has been taken of part of them.

.......................................................................................................

.......................................................................................................

.......................................................................................................

.......................................................................................................

.......................................................................................................

.......................................................................................................

.......................................................................................................

## Miscellaneous Questions

**Q1.** I have a house that I use for renting out to people and I did not buy this house with the intention to sell in the future, do I need to pay zakah on this?

**A1.** No zakah is due on the house itself. However, any income made must be added to the rest of your wealth at the end of the zakah year.

**Q2.** I have four Rolex watches, I only wear one of them usually, do I need to pay zakah on them?

**A2.** If your intention when buying them was to sell them on in the future, then you must add them to the rest of your wealth and pay zakah on them. If not, then no zakah is due.

**Q3.** I have a work pension that is not accessible until I reach the age of retirement, do I need to pay the zakah of a debt on it?

**A3.** No zakah is obligatory on it until possession of it is taken. As for private savings and accessible pensions, then zakah must be paid on them immediately.

**Q4.** Do I need to pay zakah on shares that I own?

**A4.** The value of the shares must be calculated on the day zakah is due and added to other trade items, gold, and silver.

.................................................................................................................................

.................................................................................................................................

.................................................................................................................................

.................................................................................................................................

.................................................................................................................................

.................................................................................................................................

.................................................................................................................................

.................................................................................................................................

**Q5.** I have advertised a car sale that I own for personal use, do I now need to pay zakah on it?

**A5.** No. Until the car is physically sold, no zakah is due because the basis is that it is from your original belongings.

........................................................................................................................

........................................................................................................................

........................................................................................................................

........................................................................................................................

........................................................................................................................

........................................................................................................................

........................................................................................................................

........................................................................................................................

# Bibliography


Abidin, M. A. I., 1987. *Radd al-Muhtar ala Al-Durr al-Mukhtar.* 2nd ed. Beirut: Dar Ihya al-Turath al-Arabi.

Abidin, M. A. I., 2012. *Sharh Manzumah Uqud Rasm al-Mufti.* 1st ed. Damascus: Dar al-Siddiq.

Abidin, M. A. I., Unknown. *Rasa'il Ibn Abidin, Tanbih al-Ghafil wa al-Wasnan ala Ahkam Hilal Ramadan.* 1st ed. Unknown: Unknown.

al-Ayni, B. a.-D. M. b. A., 2000. *Al-Binayah Sharh al-Hidayah.* 1st ed. Beirut: Dar al-Kutub al-Ilmiyyah.

al-Ayni, B. a.-D. M. b. A., 2011. *Nukhab al-Afkar fi Tanqih Mabani al-Akhbar fi Sharh Ma'ani al-Athar.* 1st ed. Jeddah: Dar al-Minhaj.

al-Ayni, B. a.-D. M. b. A., Unknown. *Umdah al-Qari Sharh Sahih al-Bukhari.* 1st ed. Beirut: Dar Ihya al-Turath al-Arabi.

al-Bayhaqi, A. B. A. b. a.-H., 2008. *Al-Sunan al-Kubra.* 1st ed. Cairo: Dar al-Hadith.

al-Birghivi, M. a.-D. M., 2012. *Ziyarah al-Qubur.* 6th ed. Riyadh: Maktabah al-Malik Fahd.

al-Bugha, D. M. D., 2007. *Al-Tadhhib fi Adillah Matn al-Ghayah wa-Taqrib.* 11th ed. Damascus: Dar al-Mustafa.

al-Bukhari, M. b. I., 2004. *Al-Jami' al-Sahih al-Musnad al-Mukhtasar Min Umur Rasulillah wa Sunanihi wa Ayyamihi (Sahih al-Bukhari).* 1st ed. Beirut: Dar Sader.

al-Bukhari, M. b. S. a.-S. b. M., 2004. *Al-Muit al-Burhani.* 1st ed. Beirut: Nazih Karki.

al-Dahlawi, A. b. a.-A. a.-A., 2005. *Al-Fatawa al-Tatarkhaniyyah.* 1st ed. Beirut: Dar al-Kutub al-Ilmiyyah.

al-Haddad, A. B. b. A., 1884. *Al-Jawharah al-Nayyirah ala Mukhtasar al-Quduri.* 1st ed. Multan: Maktabah Haqqaniyyah.

al-Hathami, A. b. A. B. N. a.-D., 2010. *Majma' al-Zawa'id wa Manba' al-Fawa'id.* 1st ed. Jeddah: Dar al-Minhaj.

al-Kasani, A. a.-D. A. B. b. M., 2005. *Bada'i al-Sana'i.* 1st ed. Cairo: Dar al-Hadith.

al-Lucknowi, M. A. H., 1999. *Al-Insaf fi Hukm al-I'tikaf.* 3rd ed. Beirut: Dar al-Basha'ir al-Islamiyyah.

al-Marghaynani, B. a.-D. A. b. A. B., 2006. *Al-Hidayah Sharh Bidayah al-Mubtadi.* 1st ed. Damascus: Dar al-Farfur.

al-Maturidi, M. b. M., 2005. *Ta'wilat Ahl al-Sunnah.* 1st ed. Beirut: Dar al-Kutub al-Ilmiyyah.

al-Nasafi, A. B. A. b. A., 2008. *Madarik al-Tanzil wa Haqa'iq al-Ta'wil (Tafsir al-Nasafi).* 4th ed. Damascus: Dar Ibn Kathir.

al-Nasa'i, A. b. S., 2003. *Sunan al-Nasa'i al-Sughra.* 1st ed. Damascus: Maktabah Ibn Hajar.

al-Nishapuri, M. b. a.-H. b. M., 2004. *Al-Jami' al-Sahih (Sahih Muslim).* 1st ed. Beirut: Dar Sader.

Al-Qari, N. a.-D. A. b. S., 1997. *Fath Bab al-Inayah bi Sharh al-Nuqayah.* 1st ed. Beirut: Dar al-Arqam.

al-Rumi, A. L. I. M., 2011. *Majma' al-Fawa'id li-Jam' al-Awa'id (Sharh Tuhfah al-Muluk).* 1st ed. Beirut: Dar Ibn Hazm.

al-Sarakhsi, S. a.-A. A. B. M., 2001. *Kitab al-Mabsut.* 1st ed. Beirut: Dar al-Kutub al-Ilmiyyah.

al-Shaybani, M. b. a.-H., 2012. *Al-Asl (Al-Mabsut).* 1st ed. Mardan: Maktabah al-Ahrar.

al-Shurunbulali, H. b. A., 2002. *Imdad al-Fattah Sharh Nur al-Idah.* 1 ed. Damascus: Dar al-Quba.

al-Shurunbulali, H. b. A., 2002. *Maraqi al-Falah Mukhtasar Imdad al-Fattah.* 2nd ed. Damascus: Dar al-Quba.

al-Sijistani, A. D. S. b. a.-A., 1998. *Al-Marasil.* 2nd ed. Beirut: Mu'assasah al-Risalah.

al-Sijistani, A. D. S. b. a.-A., 2010. *Kitab al-Sunan.* 3rd ed. Jeddah: Dar al-Minhaj.

al-Tabarani, S. b. A., 1985. *Al-Mu'jam al-Saghir (Al-Rawd al-Dani).* 1st ed. Beirut: Al-Maktab al-Islami.

al-Tabarani, S. b. A., 1996. *Al-Mu'jam al-Awsat.* 1st ed. Cairo: Dar al-hadith.

al-Tahawi, A. J. A., 1987. *Sharh Ma'ani al-Athar.* 2nd ed. Beirut: Dar al-Kutub al-Ilmiyyah.

al-Tahtawi, A., 2001. *Hashiyah al-Tahtawi ala Maraqi al-Falah.* 1st ed. Damascus: Dar al-Quba.

al-Tirmidhi, A. I. M. b. I., 2007. *Sunan al-Tirmidhi (Al-Jami).* 1st ed. Damascus: Dar Ibn Kathir.

al-Zayla'i, F. a.-D. U. b. A., Unknown. *Tabyin al-Haqa'iq Sharh Kanz al-Daqa'iq.* 2nd ed. Bulaq: Dar al-Kitab al-Islami.

Arabi, B. B. ed., 2004. *Al-Ikhtiyar fi Ta'lil al-Mukhtar.* 1st ed. Damascus: Dar al-Quba.

Majah, M. b. Y. a.-Q. I., 1998. *Sunan Ibn Majah.* 1st ed. Beirut: Dar al-Marifah.

Nujaym, Z. a.-D. b. I. I., 2002. *Al-Bahr al-Ra'iq Sharh Kanz al-Daqa'iq.* 1st ed. Beirut: Dar Ihya al-Turath al-Arabi.

Qutlubugha, Q. b., 2002. *Al-Tashih wa al-Tarjih ala Mukhtasar al-Quduri.* 1 ed. Beirut: Dar al-Kutub al-Ilmiyyah.

Shaybah, A. B. I. A., 2006. *Al-Musannaf.* 1st ed. Jeddah: Dar al-Minhaj.

Steingass, F., 1998. *A Comprehensive Persian-English Dictionary.* 2nd ed. Beirut: Librairie du Liban.

Taymiyyah, A. b. A. H. I., 1995. *Majmu' al-Fatawa.* 1st ed. Medina: Majma al-Malik Fahd.

Taymiyyah, T. a.-D. A. b. A. H. I., 1978. *Al-Ikhtiyarat al-Fiqhiyyah.* 1st ed. Beirut: Dar al-Marifah.

Yusuf, A., 2017. *Shedding Light on the Dawn.* 1st ed. Unknown: Nur al-Habib Productions.

# NOTES

NOTES